When FOOTBALL *Was* FOOTBALL

CARDIFF CITY

First published in 2012

A catalogue record for this book is available from the British Library

ISBN: 978-0-857331-82-3

Published by Haynes Publishing, Sparkford, Yeovil,
Somerset BA22 7JJ, UK
Tel: 01963 442030 Fax: 01963 440001
Int. tel: +44 1963 442030 Int. fax: +44 1963 440001
E-mail: sales@haynes.co.uk
Website: www.haynes.co.uk

Haynes North America Inc., 861 Lawrence Drive,
Newbury Park, California 91320, USA

Images © Mirrorpix

Creative Director: Kevin Gardner
Designed for Haynes by BrainWave

Printed and bound in the US

When
FOOTBALL *Was*
FOOTBALL

CARDIFF CITY

A Nostalgic Look at a Century of the Club

Neil Palmer

Foreword

I was born in the Grangetown area of Cardiff, and Cardiff City Football Club has run through my veins all my life. From my early schooldays of climbing over the wall into the Bob Bank for nothing and watching the likes of Ivor Allchurch, Derek Tapscott and the legendary John Charles, to my last ever game for the Bluebirds in 1985, a home defeat to Notts County, this club will always be part of me.

Throughout my career, the press have always been part of the deal when it came to playing football. I loved to read about things when they were going well at the club, and after a bad result I would probably miss the Sunday papers that weekend. I can't thank the people at the *Daily Mirror* enough for letting me be part of this wonderful book. It has brought back so many memories of my own career through its pictures, but also memories of the city of Cardiff that I love.

When it comes to hanging up your boots as a player you rely on your own memories to see you through after the crowds have gone, and with this wonderful book those memories of my beloved Cardiff City are there for every Bluebirds fan to enjoy… I hope you do.

Phil Dwyer
Cardiff City

In the Beginning
1899-1920

> " *Why wouldn't the people of Cardiff want a football club?*
>
> Bartley Wilson "

An early picture of Ninian Park from the Sloper Road End, 1910. In the distance you can see the popular bank and railway.

1899 Bartley Wilson starts the Riverside Football Club to keep the Riverside cricketers fit in the winter. **1900** Riverside play their games at Sophia Gardens, Cardiff. **1901** Cardiff becomes the biggest coal port in the world. **1905** Cardiff is given city status. **1908** A meeting by the FA grants Riverside the right to call themselves Cardiff City. **1909** Cardiff City play a friendly against Southern League Crystal Palace. **1910** Cardiff turn professional and are given land to build on at Leckwith, financed by Lord Ninian Crichton-Stuart MP. Cardiff City play Aston Villa in front of 7,000 fans at Ninian Park. **1911** Fred Stewart becomes manager. The team changes its kit colours from amber and brown to blue and white. **1912** Cardiff City are given the nickname "the Bluebirds" by supporters. Cardiff play the very first South Wales derby against Swansea Town drawing 1-1 at the Vetch Field. **1915** Nine players enlist to fight in the First World War. **1919** Seven players return from the war.

Today, Cardiff as a city is enjoying somewhat of a renascence, with building projects and investment happening all around. Over 100 years ago the town of Cardiff was experiencing the same sort of growth. It was a town on the up, and in the wake of this financial explosion Cardiff City Football Club was about to be born.

LEFT: Coal continued to become the "Black Gold" for South Wales as the mining industry struggled to keep up with the demand due to the Industrial Revolution. This meant that Cardiff had become a boomtown and it would not be long before it gained city status.

The opening of the refurbished coal exchange in Cardiff, February 1912. Cardiff became the biggest coal exporter around the world. The coal exchange was constructed in 1886 and refurbished in 1912. It was here that coal owners, ship owners and their agents would meet daily on the trading floor and set the price of coal for the whole world. During the day over 10,000 men would pass through the hall to do deals.

The first £1 million cheque (the equivalent of £78 million today) was written here in 1901 during a transaction.

LEFT: Mr Fred Stewart took over the reins at the club from player-manager Davey McDougall in 1911. Stewart came from Stockport County and brought an air of professionalism and experience to the club, attracting many great players of the day such as Billy Hardy. Stewart took the club to two FA Cup finals and also just missed out on the League Championship. The 1927 Cup final win would prove to be his finest hour. He retired from football in 1933 after being with the club for 22 years, and concentrated on his various business interests around the city before passing away in 1954.

BELOW: Captain George Latham arrived at Cardiff City in 1911 as player-coach and made Cardiff City one of the fittest teams in the league. George played for Liverpool and Southport and became Cardiff City's oldest debutant at the age of 41. During an overnight stay at Blackburn Rovers the club woke to find that players Jack Evans and Jimmy Gill had been taken ill, so with only nine fit men Harry Nash (the reserve) and George were called into action, and against the odds won 3-1. Towards the end of the game it appears that Latham was playing out on the wing and some of the Cardiff players kept hitting long balls for the 41-year-old to chase, much to his annoyance. It was his one and only appearance for the club. Latham was awarded the Military Cross for bravery in the First World War, and left the Bluebirds in 1936. He passed away three years later aged 59.

–LEGENDS–

Bartley Wilson

Bartley Wilson was a lithographic artist who had come to Cardiff to work for the Imperial Printing Company from his home in Bristol in 1895. A keen cricketer, he joined the Riverside Cricket Club and formed the Riverside Football Club in 1899 as a way of keeping the cricketers fit in the winter months.

Bartley's incredible enthusiasm to bring football to South Wales must never be forgotten. Over the years he was secretary, scout and even manager at the club. This grand old man of Cardiff City will always have a special place at the great club that he helped to create. He died in Cardiff in 1954.

COMMITTEE

Lord Ninian Crichton-Stuart

Lord Ninian Crichton-Stuart MP was the man who gave his name to Ninian Park – Cardiff City's first proper ground. He was the second son of the Marquis of Bute and he gave his financial support to the brand new club, which enabled them to move from Sophia Gardens (a temporary home) and gain the waste ground in the Leckwith area of the city to build the new ground. As a way of thanking him the club called the ground Ninian Park. Lord Ninian kicked off the very first match at the ground, a 2-1 defeat at the hands of Aston Villa in front of 7,000 fans. A keen follower of the club in the early years, Lord Ninian would lose his life in 1915. As lieutenant-colonel of the Welsh Regiment he was killed in action when leading his men on a night attack in the Battle of Loos in France; he was 32 years old. Lord Ninian was shot by a sniper at midnight on 2nd October 1915 as he peered over the trench to watch the enemy. Out of the 842 members of his regiment, who left South Wales to fight in the Great War, only 30 returned. In 2007 his granddaughter Marietta took some soil from Ninian Park and took it to France to scatter on the spot where he was killed so that the City would always be with him. There is a statue of this brave man in Gorsedd Gardens, Cardiff.

Here he is pictured at Sophia Gardens (with cigarette) watching Cardiff in 1908, sat in the committee seats.

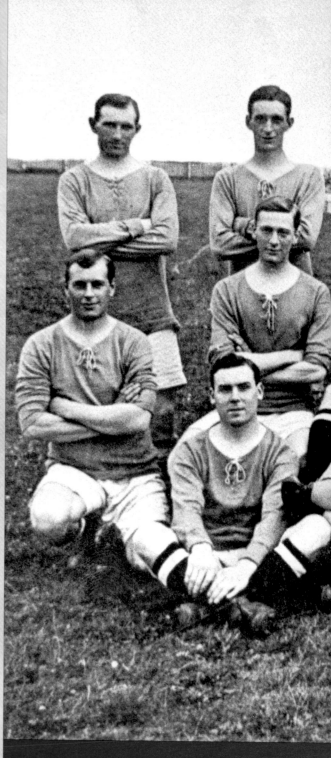

The New Theatre, Cardiff where the classic children's play *The Blue Bird*, by Belgian playwright Maurice Maeterlinck, was playing in 1909. It is believed that the popularity of the play and the fact that the Bluebird was a symbol of happiness led fans to replace the team's nicknames "the Cardiffians" and "the Citizens" with the nickname "the Bluebirds". This would also coincide with the club changing their kit from the Riverside colours of amber and brown to blue and white.

Cardiff City FC 1913/14 season, Southern League Division One. The team guided by Fred Stewart would finish 10th this season.

The Roaring Twenties
1920-1929

Back at Cardiff – the official photograph showing the whole squad and officials with the cup.

The 1920s would prove to be a defining decade for the Bluebirds. They started it as the new boys in the league and finished it one of the best teams in the country after featuring in two Wembley Cup finals and just missing out on the Championship.

1920 Cardiff City join the Football League Division Two. 25,000 fans see the first home league game against Clapton Orient. Cardiff win promotion to Division One. **1923** Cardiff miss out on the league title by 0.024 of a goal; no other club to this day would miss out by such a narrow margin. **1924** Cardiff City become the first British club to provide both captains in a full international when Jimmy Blair's Scotland takes on Fred Keenor's Wales at Ninian Park. **1925** Cardiff lose 1-0 to Sheffield United in the FA Cup final at Wembley. Jimmy Nelson is the first ever Cardiff City player to be sent off. **1926** Cardiff suffer their worst ever defeat 11-2 to Sheffield United. **1927** Cardiff become the only team to take the cup out of England by beating Arsenal 1-0. **1928** Hughie Ferguson scores five as Cardiff beat Burnley 7-1. **1929** Ferguson leaves for Dundee. Cardiff City are relegated to Division Two.

–LEGENDS–

Hughie Ferguson

Hughie Ferguson was the Scotsman who will live forever in the hearts of Cardiff City fans. Born in Glasgow, Hughie started his career with local side Parkhead Juniors. He joined Motherwell in 1916 and quickly became one of the hottest properties in football netting 284 goals for Motherwell.

In 1925 Ferguson came south of the border and joined Cardiff City for a massive £5,000, just £1,000 less than the British record. Motherwell's loss was certainly Cardiff's gain and he wasted no time in repaying the massive transfer fee, scoring on his debut in a 5-2 victory over Leicester City. Ferguson's record at Cardiff City was phenomenal with 93 goals in 139 appearances including five in a 7-1 drubbing of Burnley.

But he will always be remembered for the goal that won the FA Cup for the Bluebirds in 1927. Hughie admitted that it was not one of his better goals as his shot towards the Arsenal goal on that April afternoon at Wembley was clumsily fumbled by the Gunners' Welsh goalkeeper Dan Lewis, which resulted in the ball spinning off Lewis' chest into the net.

In 1929, suffering from a loss of form and Cardiff City strapped for cash, the Bluebirds sold Ferguson to Dundee for £500. Hughie struggled at Dens Park and soon became the target of the angry Dundee fans who could not believe that this once great striker appeared to be having trouble even running for a ball. The mental anguish of these events led Hughie to take his own life by gassing himself after training at Dundee's ground. He was 32 years of age and left a wife and two children. It was a tragic end for somebody who even today is only one of a few British footballers to have scored 350 league goals. It later transpired that Hughie had a tumour in his brain, which could explain his loss of form at Dundee.

When Cardiff City reached the 2008 FA Cup final Hughie's family were invited to the game as guests of the club in recognition of this great Bluebird of yesteryear.

FOOTBALL –STATS–

Hughie Ferguson

Name: Hugh Ferguson

Born: 1898

Died: 1930

Playing Career: Motherwell, Cardiff City, Dundee

Cardiff City Appearances: 139

Cardiff City Goals: 93

Fred Keenor battles it out with Arsenal's Jimmy Brain in the 1927 final.

BELOW: Cardiff City would make history in 1924 when they became the first British club to provide both captains in a full international as Fred Keenor led his Wales team against Jimmy Blair's Scotland side at Ninian Park. Both players would only be given international shirts, as was the custom of the day, so the shorts and socks are Cardiff City's.

–LEGENDS–

Fred Keenor

Even though some tremendous footballers have pulled on the blue shirt of Cardiff City, none have come close to Fred Keenor. Fred was a real man's man; respected by friend or foe he took Cardiff City to two FA Cup finals and to the verge of the First Division title. This no-nonsense defender was certainly made of different stock than most of today's footballers. Keenor came to the attention of his hometown club Cardiff City whilst playing in the very first schoolboy international between England and Wales in 1907. Cardiff signed him on amateur forms in 1911 then full professional forms in 1913.

With the outbreak of the First World War Fred, like so many of his fellow footballers, joined up to fight and found himself in the trenches. Fred was injured twice during hostilities in France but he returned to his beloved Cardiff City after the war where he incredibly led them to the FA Cup final in 1925 against Sheffield United. After Cardiff's 1-0 defeat he told supporters he would take them there again and would win the cup, which he did on St George's Day in 1927 when Cardiff City beat the mighty Arsenal to take the cup out of England and home to Wales. Keenor's leadership qualities were not only appreciated by Cardiff but by his country also, who he played for 31 times.

Fred played his last game for the Bluebirds in 1931 and moved to Crewe Alexandra. He stayed at Crewe for three years before returning to Wales where he died in 1972 aged 78. He was the greatest Bluebird of all.

FOOTBALL –STATS–

Fred Keenor

Name: Frederick Keenor

Born: 1894

Died: 1972

Playing Career: Cardiff City, Crewe Alexandra, Wales

Cardiff City Appearances: 446

Cardiff City Goals: 19

Wales Appearances: 32

Wales Goals: 2

Fred Keenor holds Mascot "Trixie" the cat as they arrive in England's capital ahead of the 1927 Cup final. In the build-up to Cardiff's FA Cup third-round tie at Bolton Wanderers, the players relaxed with a round of golf at the Royal Birkdale Golf Club. During the round some of the players noticed that a small black kitten was following them. They took this to be a lucky omen and Hughie Ferguson was dispatched to find the owner to try and fix a deal that would mean the players keeping the animal. Hughie struck a deal where they could keep the kitten provided that they would supply the owner with a ticket should they make the final. The team christened the kitten Trixie and took it to every Cup-tie. She remained at Ninian Park until her death in 1939.

The Welsh Invasion of London

It is thought that over 60,000 Cardiff City fans made the trip to the capital to see the game.

Cardiff City players fool around in Fred Keenor's car prior to the Cup-tie against Bolton Wanderers.

Two Cardiff City fans ready for the game at Wembley.

LEFT: Fans climb the gates of Horse Guards Parade to get a glimpse of the changing of the guard.

BELOW: Fans are in a good mood ready for the big game in the Whitechapel area of London.

In this crowd scene policemen are forced to climb over people to reach the back of the terrace.

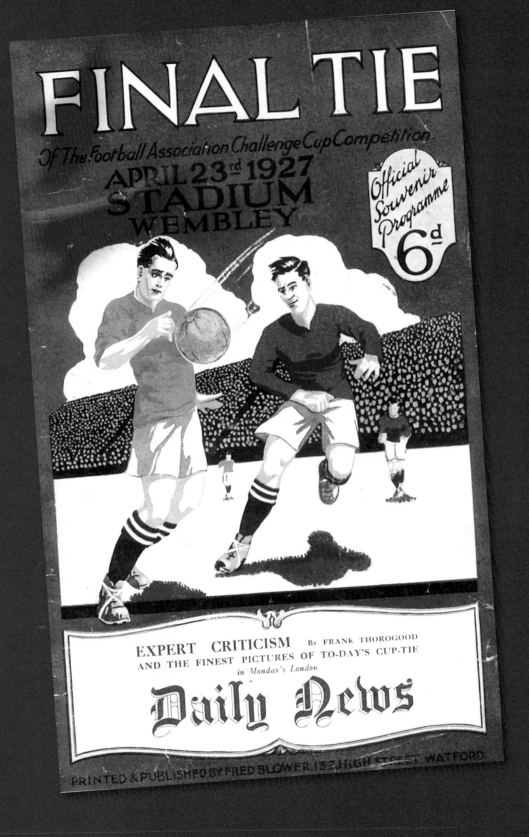

The Cup final programme.

The game midway through the first half. The match was the very first game broadcast live on the radio. The BBC *Radio Times* gave away a free sheet with the pitch marked out and numbered so people could follow where the ball and players were. The goalmouth was marked square one, which apparently is where the saying "Back to square one" originates.

27

ABOVE: Captain Fred Keenor introduces George McLachlan to King George V before kick-off.

RIGHT: Fred Keenor shakes Arsenal captain Charles Buchan's hand.

ABOVE: Cardiff City's Tom Sloan clears the danger with Cardiff's Tom Watson behind.

LEFT: Arsenal keeper Don Lewis fumbles the shot as Cardiff's Len Davis looks on.

A section of the Wembley crowd.

Len Davis watches as Hughie Ferguson's shot is fumbled by Arsenal's keeper Lewis to crawl agonizingly across the line. Lewis later blamed his brand new goalkeeping shirt as one of the reasons that it slipped out of his grasp, claiming the ball spun off the shirt. Out of superstition, to this day Arsenal keepers have never worn a "new shirt" in any final.

ABOVE: Cardiff City fans' reaction to the final whistle.

LEFT: Billy Hardy tries to get off the pitch at Wembley to join his team-mates on the steps of the Royal Box to receive the cup.

The Cardiff City team, led by captain Fred Keenor, receive the cup from King George V.

Some of the victorious Cardiff City team pose for a photo with the cup in the Wembley dressing room after the 1-0 win against Arsenal. From left to right: Hughie Ferguson, Tom Sloan, Fred Keenor, Ernie Curtis and Tom Watson.

Billy Hardy takes a drink of champagne from the cup as Fred Keenor has a cigarette to celebrate. Cardiff reserve team manager Tom Pirie holds the lid of the cup, while in the background manager Fred Stewart talks to a dignitary.

DAILY MIRROR

£100 FREE CROSS-WORD COMPETITION: SEE PAGE 16

THE DAILY PICTURE newspaper WITH THE LARGEST NET SALE

No. 7,316   TUESDAY, APRIL 26, 1927   One Penny

24 PAGES

CARDIFF CHEERS CAPTORS OF THE ENGLISH CUP

LOVERS FOUND SHOT DEAD IN A CAR

ABOVE: How the *Daily Mirror* reported the victorious Cardiff City team's return to Wales.

> *I have never seen Cardiff so full of people.*
>
> Fred Keenor on bringing the cup back to South Wales in 1927

ABOVE: Chaos as Fred Keenor tries to get to the team coach but the fans want to get to Fred Keenor and the cup!

RIGHT: Keenor leans out of the team coach surrounded by fans as the driver tries to get the team kit onto the roof.

37

The boys of 1927. Never to be forgotten. Left to right, back row: George Latham (trainer), Jimmy Nelson, Tom Farquharson, Tom Watson and George McLachlan. Middle row: Tom Sloan, Sam Irving, Fred Keenor (captain), Billy Hardy and Len Davies. Front row: Ernie Curtis and Hughie Ferguson.

Fred, with former Arsenal player Bob John, pictured in 1969 looking at the 1927 programme with a picture of the goal that won the FA Cup behind them.

The Rollercoaster Years
1930-1970

Billy James, in later years, chatting to ground staff at Ninian Park.

1931 Cardiff are relegated to Division Three South. 1932 Manager Fred Stewart resigns. Cardiff apply to the Football League for re-election. 1936 After a break-in at the club, thieves set fire to the grandstand at Ninian Park. 1938 Billy James joins the club as a promising schoolboy. 1939 The outbreak of the Second World War. 1945 Cardiff lose 10-1 to Moscow Dynamo in a friendly. 1946 Cardiff win Division Three South. 1947 Cardiff finish fifth in Division Two. 1948 56,000 fans cram into Ninian Park to see Cardiff lose 1-0 to Tottenham Hotspur. 1949 Cardiff finish fourth in the league. 1952 Cardiff clinch promotion to Division One. 1953 Record attendance of 57,893 see Cardiff City against Arsenal at Ninian Park. 1954 Cardiff break their transfer record by paying £30,000 for Trevor Ford from Sunderland. 1955 Youngster Neil O'Halloran scores a hat-trick of headers on his debut against Charlton Athletic. 1956 Cardiff are relegated to Division Two. 1957 The club finish 15th in Division Two. 1958 Bill Jones takes over as manager. 1959/60 Cardiff City are promoted to Division One under manager Bill Jones. 1961 Cardiff pay £28,000 for Welsh international Mel Charles from Arsenal. 1962 Cardiff are relegated to Division Two. 1963 John Charles signs from Italian club Roma for £25,000. 1964 Scottish-born Jimmy Scoular becomes manager of Cardiff City. 1965 Sixteen-year-old John Toshack scores on his Bluebirds debut. 1966 Cardiff City finish 20th in Division Two. 1967 Brian Clark signs from Huddersfield Town. 1968 John Toshack becomes the Second Division's leading goalscorer with 23 goals. 1969/70 Cardiff finish seventh in Division Two.

The Thirties

After the success of the Twenties, the Thirties would prove to be a miserable time for supporters and those connected with the club. The writing was on the wall with the transfer of Hughie Ferguson and his tragic death at the start of the decade, and Fred Keenor had flown the nest and moved to Crewe Alexandra in 1931. Coupled with an ageing side it seems incredible that only six years after lifting the cup at Wembley the club had to seek re-election to the Football League.

Numerous reasons were put forward for the decline of the club but many felt that the directors choosing to spend the money from the FA Cup to improve the ground rather than investing in the team was the main cause. It's a difficult choice to make even in today's mega-rich game.

Billy James

Billy was destined for great things. He joined Cardiff City as a schoolboy, and Cardiff manager Cyril Spiers insisted on him joining the first team as soon as possible. He made his debut against Notts County in 1941, and was capped for Wales. Many thought he would be one of the greatest inside-forwards of his generation. He joined the army at 18 years of age and, with his regiment, went to Java.

Billy was taken as a prisoner of war for four years by the Japanese in Java. As a result of life in the camp Billy's sight became affected and on his return to Wales he was forced to give up his career.

Like many teams throughout the war years Cardiff would try to keep playing football matches by arranging friendlies as the league was suspended. This could well mean players from other sides turning out for the Bluebirds so the club could fill fixtures. Some of these players would play one game and some even became regulars for the club. Cardiff's most famous guest player was Bill Shankly who played for the club in the 1942/43 season. Shankly played one game for the Bluebirds, a match against local side Lovell's Athletic in 1942. He apparently refused any other offers as his match fee was 30 shillings (£1.50) and he found out that the Lovell's players were paid £5 a game.

43

The Forties

With the end of the Second World War a new era was beginning, not only in Europe, but also in Cardiff for the Bluebirds. The club started to rely on younger local lads, and with new optimism they started the climb back up the league.

LEFT: Cardiff in action at White Hart Lane going down 2-0 to Spurs in the 1949 season.

Hands Across Europe

In 1945 the great Moscow Dynamo toured Britain playing Chelsea, Arsenal, West Ham, Glasgow Rangers and Cardiff City. As the Russians wore blue, Cardiff turned out in red shirts. The game was watched by 31,000 fans at Ninian Park but unfortunately the Russians were far too good for their Welsh counterparts and won the game 10-1.

ABOVE: Both teams line up for the friendly in November 1945.

BELOW: The Cardiff team present the Moscow players with miners lamps as a way of welcoming them to Wales.

–LEGENDS–

Alf Sherwood

Alf Sherwood will always be known as Mr Dependable to the Cardiff fans. Ex-minor Alf signed for the club in 1941 and played over 100 wartime games for Cardiff. In 1946 he made his debut against Norwich City at full-back and seemed to be there forever. A Welsh international with 41 caps to his name, Sherwood was known as a tough-tackling full-back who gave everything for the Bluebirds. A great captain and leader he possessed traits that would have made him worth millions in today's game. Alf left Cardiff City in 1956 and joined Newport County where he played a further 200 games before his retirement in 1961 aged 38.

ABOVE: Cardiff City captain Alf Sherwood introduces Field Marshall Viscount Montgomery (Monty) to the Cardiff players in 1953. Here he is shaking hands with Cardiff's Stan Montgomery as Frank Dudley and George Edwards look on.

BELOW: Alf Sherwood in the 1950/51 side. Alf is in the front row, second on the right.

> "The most difficult opponent I ever faced."
>
> Stanley Matthews

FOOTBALL –STATS–

Alf Sherwood

Name: Alfred Sherwood

Born: 1923

Died: 1990

Playing Career: Cardiff City, Newport County, Wales

Cardiff City Appearances: 379

Cardiff City Goals: 15

Wales Appearances: 41

Wales Goals: 0

The Fifties

The decade started with promotion and ended with promotion to Division One. Along the way the Cardiff public were to witness some of the club's greatest players.

LEFT: Crowds of supporters gather along Sloper Road on their way to Ninian Park for a home game. The average weekly wage at the time was £6, and with admission to the ground being 2/6 or 12 and a half pence, the average crowd for the Bluebirds in the Fifties was 25,000. The supporters obviously thought it was money well spent!

Cardiff City's 1951/52 promotion winning team. Back row, left to right: Walter Robins (trainer), Roley Williams, Stan Montgomery, Cyril Spiers (manager), Ron Howells, Glyn Williams, Ron Stitfall and Doug Blair. Front row, left to right: Mike Tiddy, Ken Chisholm, Bobby McLaughlin, Alf Sherwood (captain), George Edwards, Wilf Grant and Derrick Sullivan.

Derek in the thick of the action against Chelsea as Mel Charles looks on.

"

The best bit of business I ever did.

Bill Jones (Cardiff manager 1958–1962)

"

Derek in full flow against Leyton Orient at Ninian Park.

–LEGENDS–

Derek Tapscott

Derek Tapscott was the South Wales lad that got away. Derek played Southern League football for Barry Town and it was there that he was spotted and taken to Arsenal right under the noses of Cardiff City. Tapscott had five seasons at Highbury in which he scored 61 goals in 119 games. Cardiff were languishing near the bottom of Division Two when manager Bill Jones paid £10,000 for the inside-forward. As it turned out Jones would later state that it was the best bit of business he ever did, as with Tapscott upfront the club pulled away from the bottom of the division. Tapscott was instrumental in Cardiff's promotion season of 1960 as he contributed 20 goals. Capped by Wales he will always be remembered as a brave goal poacher that Cardiff could have had for nothing. Derek finished his Cardiff career in 1965 when he joined Newport County. He died in 2008; Cardiff fans will always have a special place in their hearts for "Tappy".

FOOTBALL –STATS–

Derek Tapscott

Name: Derek Tapscott

Born: 1932

Died: 2008

Playing Career: Arsenal, Cardiff City, Newport County, Wales

Cardiff City Appearances: 234

Cardiff City Goals: 101

Wales Appearances: 14

Wales Goals: 4

Baker heads away danger.

–LEGENDS–

Colin Baker

Colin Baker is without doubt the greatest ever wing-half to play for Cardiff City. He is also a man on a very short list: a Welshman who has played in a World Cup. Baker played for Wales in the 1958 tournament in Sweden as the gallant Welsh side reached the quarter-finals only to be knocked out by the Brazilians and a youngster called Pelé. Born in Cardiff, Baker made his Cardiff City debut on the final day of the 1953/54 season against Sheffield Wednesday. He soon established himself in the Cardiff line-up. He possessed a fine shot with either foot and his long-range efforts made him a firm favourite with the Ninian Park faithful. Colin played for the Bluebirds up until 1965 before retiring from the game.

" *Colin is the perfect wing-half.*

Jimmy Murphy, Wales manager, 1958 World Cup "

FOOTBALL –STATS–
Colin Baker

Name: Colin Baker

Born: 1934

Playing Career: Cardiff City, Wales

Cardiff City Appearances: 361

Cardiff City Goals: 20

Wales Appearances: 7

Wales Goals: 0

LEFT: The groundsman pours Colin a cup of tea as the other Cardiff players look on after training in 1958.

BELOW: Colin in action against Rotherham, 1959.

–LEGENDS–

Trevor Ford

Trevor Ford would not have been out of place in today's modern game: immaculately dressed off the field and a real superstar on it. Although he was not at Cardiff City long he certainly made his mark. Trevor started his career at rivals Swansea Town but soon joined Aston Villa for £10,000 in 1947. After successful seasons at Villa he joined Sunderland in 1950 for a fee of £30,000 and went on to score 67 goals in 108 games for the Black Cats. Cardiff City broke their transfer record to bring Ford to Ninian Park for £30,000. Ford was a real superstar in the Cardiff team, but in 1956 things at Ninian turned sour and after a poor run of results manager Trevor Morris told Ford that he would be playing wide right to which Ford refused. From that day Fordy's days were numbered and he left Cardiff later that year. Revelations about illegal payments in his Sunderland days led Ford to receive a three-year ban from British football so he went and played in Holland with PSV Eindhoven, before ending his career at Newport County. Cardiff fans will always remember the bustling centre-forward who took no prisoners and created havoc for centre-halves in his day.

> *He was a superstar in every way.*
>
> Colin Baker, Cardiff City, talking about Trevor

FOOTBALL –STATS–

Trevor Ford

Name: Trevor Ford

Born: 1923

Died: 2003

Playing Career: Swansea Town, Aston Villa, Sunderland, Cardiff City, PSV Eindhoven, Newport County, Wales

Cardiff City Appearances: 110

Cardiff City Goals: 59

Wales Appearances: 38

Wales Goals: 23

LEFT: Trevor captains Cardiff City in the 1956 Welsh Cup final. He is pictured here with opposing Swansea captain and Welsh great Ivor Allchurch who would later join the Bluebirds.

Trademark Ford as he crashes a diving header towards goal in the 4-1 victory over Leeds United in 1956.

BELOW: Trevor "roughing up" Swansea keeper Johnny King in front of 36,000 fans in the 1956 Welsh Cup final as Gerry Hitchins runs on.

Cardiff City star Gerry Hitchens in action against Spurs at White Hart Lane in a 1-1 draw. Hitchens signed from Kidderminster Harriers for £1,500 in 1955 and built up a formidable partnership with Trevor Ford, which ended in 1957 when Aston Villa paid £22,000 for Hitchens, who would go on to have success in Italy with Inter Milan, Atlanta, Torino and Cagliari. He also played for England in the 1962 World Cup in Chile.

Cardiff City's Ron Stitfall looks to make a tackle in the game against Doncaster Rovers.

Ron was at the club for over 20 years from 1942–1964. Cardiff born and bred, Ron could play anywhere and certainly would when asked. But it was at full-back where he proved that there was not many better. He served Cardiff well and played over 400 games for the club.

The 1955 Bluebird side managed by Trevor Morris. They held their own in English football's elite before relegation to Division Two beckoned in the 1956/57 season. Back row, left to right: Kirtley, Tiddy, Frowen, Howells, Harrington and Jones. Front row: Davies, Stockin, Rutter, Mcseveney, Hitchens.

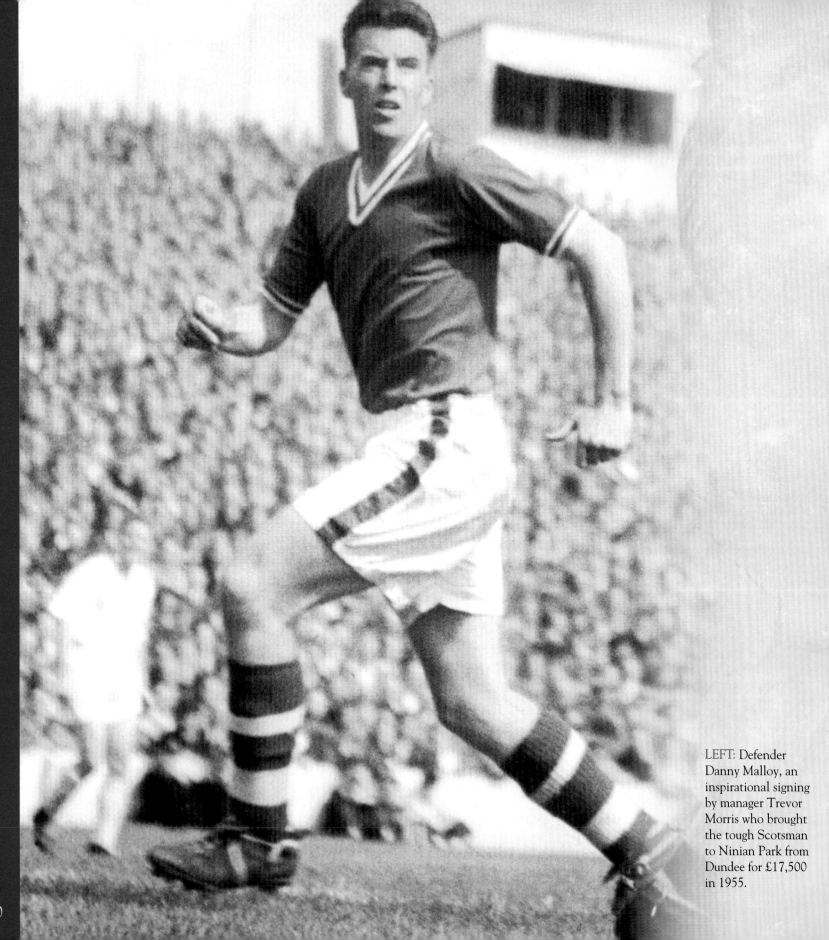

LEFT: Defender
Danny Malloy, an
inspirational signing
by manager Trevor
Morris who brought
the tough Scotsman
to Ninian Park from
Dundee for £17,500
in 1955.

What a Debut

Youngster Neil O'Halloran scored a hat-trick of headers on his Cardiff City debut against Charlton Athletic at Ninian Park, 10th December 1955.

RIGHT: Neil O'Halloran scoring one of his three goals on his debut against Charlton Athletic.

Bill Jones' 1958 side led by Ron Stitfall (front row centre). The nucleus of this side would achieve promotion to the top flight in the 1959/60 season, after finishing second in Division Two behind Aston Villa, despite scoring 90 goals that season.

Promotion to the Big Time

Cardiff City keeper Ron Nicholls catches the ball from an Aston Villa attack.

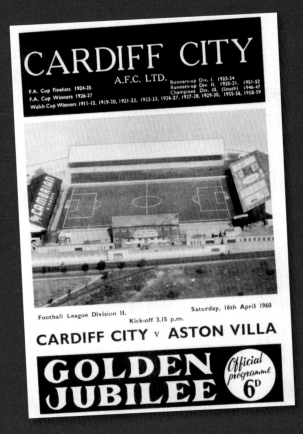

A programme of the 1959/60 game between Cardiff City and Aston Villa. If Cardiff won this game they could clinch promotion to Division One. 55,000 fans crammed into a bursting Ninian Park to see the Bluebirds win 1-0 with a goal from Graham Moore.

Aston Villa keeper Nigel Sims denies Cardiff City's Colin Hudson.

ABOVE: Cardiff City captain Danny Malloy, with cigarette in hand, addresses the Cardiff fans from the grandstand after Cardiff's 1-0 win against Aston Villa, securing the Welsh club promotion to Division One.

RIGHT: Cardiff City's Alan Durban challenges Derby County's goalkeeper Mitchell during Cardiff's 2-0 win in 1959. Cardiff would later sell Durban to Derby County for £10,000 in 1963, where he would become a valued member of Brian Clough's title-winning team. Durban would later return to Ninian Park as manager in 1984.

BELOW: Danny Malloy autographs a souvenir *South Wales Echo* in the dressing room at Ninian Park after the team's game against Plymouth Argyle. Cardiff had already clinched promotion. Watching are, left to right: Colin Baker; 14-year-old fan Jeffery Clement, 10-year-old fan Peter Greenwood; Alec Milne; 14-year-old fan Phillip Lloyd; and Malloy.

The Sixties

Cardiff started the Swinging Sixties in football's top flight but spent the rest of the decade in the Second Division. Despite this, they were able to attract some of Welsh football's greatest names. People like John Charles, Mel Charles and Ivor Allchurch all joined the Bluebirds and, although some of their better days may have been at other clubs, it was a real treat for the fans and it seemed fitting that these national heroes should come and play for the principality's capital club. These legends of Welsh football, brought in from other clubs, were not the only players worshipped by the Cardiff City fans as the club started to produce its own idols in the shape of Phil Dwyer and John Toshack.

Cardiff City players relaxing after a Turkish bath at the Empire pool, Cardiff. Left to right: Barrie Hole, Trevor Peck, Steve Gammon, John Charles, Derek Tapscott and Alan Harrington.

–LEGENDS–

John Toshack

When 16-year-old John Toshack came off the substitutes bench against Leyton Orient in 1965 Cardiff City announced to the world they had found a gem. Toshack scored in the 3-1 victory and he found his way into the Bluebird supporters' hearts. The goals kept coming for the young Toshack and it was inevitable that big clubs would come calling, and they did not come any bigger than Liverpool who signed the youngster for £110,000 in 1970, much to the anger of the Bluebird fans who had grown to love the partnership Toshack had developed with Brian Clark up front.

Toshack would go on to win every honour with Liverpool and also establish himself as a regular with Wales. In 1977, after leaving Liverpool, he "offered" his services to his hometown club but his offer was rejected. He went on to become rivals Swansea City's player-manager, taking them from the Fourth Division to the First in successive seasons. Toshack scored the last league goal of his career against Cardiff at the Grangetown End at Ninian Park in the 1983 derby game almost 20 years after he scored his first league goal for the Bluebirds at the same end.

The lad from Cardiff would go on to manage at the highest level throughout Europe, taking charge of the likes of Sporting Lisbon, Real Zaragoza and Real Madrid, as well as the Welsh national side.

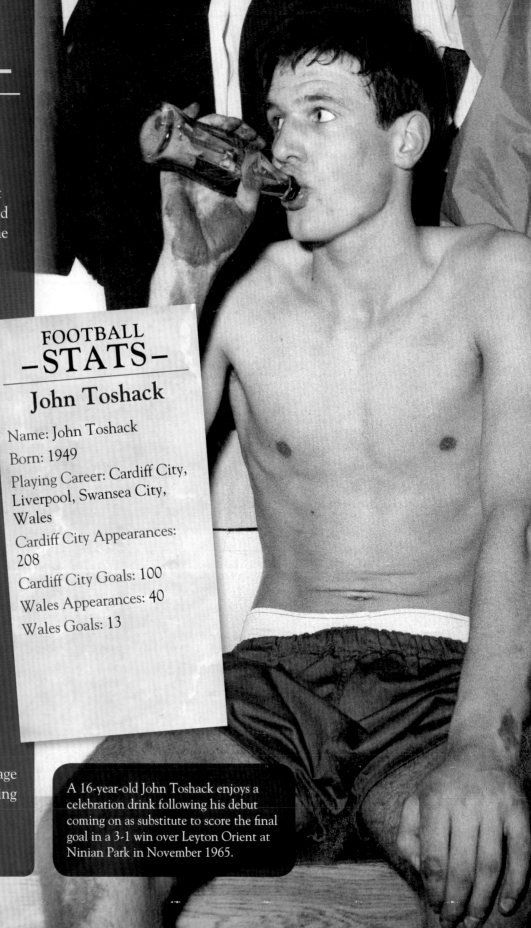

FOOTBALL –STATS–

John Toshack

Name: John Toshack
Born: 1949
Playing Career: Cardiff City, Liverpool, Swansea City, Wales
Cardiff City Appearances: 208
Cardiff City Goals: 100
Wales Appearances: 40
Wales Goals: 13

A 16-year-old John Toshack enjoys a celebration drink following his debut coming on as substitute to score the final goal in a 3-1 win over Leyton Orient at Ninian Park in November 1965.

Crystal Palace keeper John Jackson collects the ball as John Toshack closes in on goal in a 4-0 defeat for the Bluebirds at Ninian Park.

John had everything.

Brian Clark

LEFT: John Toshack and strike partner Brian Clark in action against Blackburn Rovers at Ninian Park in 1969.

Toshack said of Clark "He taught me everything I needed to be a striker."

RIGHT: John Toshack, with his mentor Bill Shankly, after leaving Cardiff City for Shankly's Liverpool in 1970.

The greatest footballer of his generation and, arguably, Wales' greatest footballer, John Charles in Cardiff City colours. Charles was a footballing legend when he arrived at Ninian Park, and although his greatest days may have been behind him, he still gave everything for the Bluebirds. Although manager George Swindin was not keen on buying Charles due to his age, Swindin was overruled by the board who paid the £25,000 that Italian giants Roma were looking for. The Cardiff fans loved having the "Gentle Giant" in the side and many wondered what would have happened if Leeds United had accepted Cardiff City's offer of £40,000 for the player in 1953. Charles could play anywhere. England forward Nat Lofthouse said he was the best centre-half he'd ever played against, whilst England centre-half Billy Wright said he was the best centre-forward that he had ever played against. Big John played 66 times for Cardiff scoring 19 goals in a two-year spell.

ABOVE: John Charles signs for Cardiff City, watched by manager George Swindin, following his £25,000 move from Italian club Roma in 1963.

RIGHT: Charles looks unhappy after Charlton's Eddie Firmani scores at the Valley, 1963.

ABOVE: Mel Charles in action against Swansea in 1962. He signed for Cardiff after coming from Arsenal in a deal worth £28,000 in 1961. Charles scored 119 goals for the Bluebirds in a three-year spell. Always in the shadow of his brother John, Mel was a much better player than he was given credit for. He was voted best centre-half of the 1958 World Cup in Sweden. He left the Bluebirds after a clear-out by manager Jimmy Scoular in 1965.

Ivor Allchurch signed for the Bluebirds in 1962 for £18,000 from Newcastle United. He was the "Golden Boy" of Welsh football for his looks and wonderful ball-playing skills. Cardiff fans only had him for three years but never forgot him. It was said that when he was attacking the Grangetown End he could send 10,000 people the wrong way with a body swerve.

ABOVE: The great Ivor Allchurch leaping ahead of Newcastle defender John McGrath to score against the Magpies in 1964.

LEFT: Ivor Allchurch leaving Ninian Park and heading across Sloper Road for training.

73

74

Cardiff City's very own Galacticos circa 1964. Back row, left to right: Gareth Williams, Barrie Hole, Don Murray, John Charles, Mel Charles, Trevor Peck, Steve Gammon and Ernie Curtis (trainer). Front row: Dick Scott, Greg Farrell, Dillwyn John, Graham Vearncombe, Ivor Allchurch and Peter Rodrigues.

Cardiff City keeper Graham Vearncombe dives at the feet of young Sunderland striker Brian Clough as Sunderland beat Cardiff 2-1 at Roker Park in 1962.

ABOVE: Cardiff City players celebrate beating Hereford United 4-1 at Ninian Park to win the 1968 Welsh Cup.

BELOW: Cardiff players meet up at Cardiff Central railway station before their 1968 end-of-season tour to Australia and New Zealand. They played 14 games and only lost once.

European Nights
1964-1993

Cardiff were certainly no strangers to European football. As early as 1924 they toured Czechoslovakia, Austria and Germany, where they played Sparta Prague, Vienna, Borussia Dortmund and SV Hamburg. After the trip the players commented on the skill of the continentals – but the food in Europe certainly did not win any fans. And the club's exploits in 1945 against Moscow Dynamo were well documented.

With the installation of floodlights at Ninian Park in 1960, as well as the Welsh Cup becoming a passage into Europe with entry to the Cup Winners' Cup, it was always hoped that Cardiff would have some wonderful European nights. Little did they know at the time that those nights would be etched in the memories of those fans that were there and even those that were not.

Supporters celebrate Brian Clark's goal against Real Madrid. The result would be the talk of football for years. Cardiff's next game was away to Blackburn Rovers in the league. Blackburn made them run out at Ewood Park first and the whole of the crowd stood on their feet and applauded Cardiff's achievement.

1964 Cardiff beat Danish side Esbjerg 1-0 on aggregate in Cardiff's first European game. Cardiff beat Sporting Lisbon 2-1. Cardiff lose 3-2 on aggregate to Real Zaragoza in the quarter-finals. 1965 Cardiff lose an ill-tempered two-legged affair against the Belgium side Standard Liege 3-1 on aggregate. 1967 The Bluebirds beat Dutch side NAC Breda 5-2 on aggregate. 1968 Cardiff beat Moscow Torpedo 1-0 to reach the semi-finals. 43,000 fans cram into Ninian Park to see Cardiff lose 2-3 in the home leg against SV Hamburg to go out of the competition 4-3 on aggregate. 1969 The Bluebirds play FC Porto in the first round. 1970 Cardiff demolish the French side Nantes 5-1 at Ninian Park. 1971 Brian Clark scores to beat Real Madrid 1-0 at Ninian Park. Cardiff lose 2-0 against Real Madrid at the Bernabeu in front of 65,000 fans. 1972 Cardiff play Dynamo Berlin but lose on penalties. 1973 Cardiff are knocked out 2-1 by Sporting Lisbon. 1974 The Bluebirds are beaten 6-1 on aggregate by Turkish club Ferencvaros. 1976 Cardiff lose to Dynamo Tblisi 3-1 on aggregate in the first round. 1977 FK Austria Memphis beat Cardiff City 1-0 on aggregate. 1988 Cardiff lose 6-1 to Aarhus. 1992 The Bluebirds lose 3-1 on aggregate to Austrian side Admira Wacker. 1993 Cardiff lose 8-3 on aggregate to Standard Liege in their last European adventure.

Friendly European Relations

ABOVE: Cardiff City players wave goodbye, heading for another European adventure in the European Cup Winners' Cup.

ABOVE: Carvalho carries Tapscott off the pitch, whether he likes it or not, after a goalmouth incident.

BELOW: A battered Derek Tapscott in the Cardiff City dressing room after the game in Lisbon.

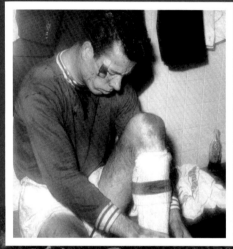

ABOVE: An ill-tempered match between Cardiff City and Sporting Lisbon in 1964. Lisbon were the cup holders and Cardiff were in the Second Division, yet the Bluebirds won in Portugal 2-1 then drew 0-0 at Ninian Park, thus knocking the holders out and making Europe sit up and notice them.

BELOW: Sporting Lisbon keeper Carvalho hurls himself at battered striker Derek Tapscott in Portugal.

BELOW RIGHT: Cardiff City v Standard Liege, 1969. Cardiff's John Charles goes down injured following an incident that led to a mass brawl between players.

LEFT: Pictured left to right are Peter King, Don Murray, Barrie Jones, Ronnie Bird, Bryn Jones and John Toshack in the dressing room after beating Moscow Torpedo 1-0. Cardiff won in Tashkent, which was 2,000 miles from Torpedo's Moscow home and on the Chinese border. The game was played there due to the Russian capital being frozen solid. It was the longest trip ever undertaken . by a football club in a European competition and resulted in a tremendous display by the club.

LEFT: Mrs Gloria Davies, along with secretary Graham Keenor, deal with ticket applications for Cardiff's European Cup Winners' Cup semi-final against SV Hamburg at Ninian Park.

BELOW: The SV Hamburg keeper can only watch in agony as Cardiff City's Brian Harris' header hits the net in the semi-final second leg in front of 43,000 fans.

Cardiff City fans run on to the pitch to congratulate captain
Brian Harris after scoring his goal.

Celebration on the Bob Bank as Cardiff City's Norman Dean scores the Bluebirds' first goal in the European Cup Winners' Cup semi-final. The joy turned to tears as, with the game poised at 2-2 (3-3 on aggregate), SV Hamburg scored with the last kick of the match to make it 3-2 on the night and to put the Germans through 4-3 on aggregate.

A special moment for striker Brian Clark and every Cardiff City fan as Clark scores one of Cardiff's most famous goals: the header that beat the mighty Real Madrid in 1971. Clark said later: "It was the highlight of my career and a night I will never forget."

The Cardiff City team at Rhoose Airport, Cardiff, ready to board the plane to Madrid for the second leg of their European Cup Winners' Cup quarter-final at the Bernabeu Stadium. Unfortunately, after a gallant effort, the Bluebirds were beaten 2-0 in front of 70,000 and went out 2-1 on aggregate, but their achievement will always be remembered.

RIGHT: Cardiff striker Anthony Bird scores one of his two goals in Cardiff's last foray into Europe, with a 5-2 defeat against Belgium side Standard Liege, in the 1993 Cup Winners' Cup first round. Bird, a product of the Cardiff City youth team, was released by the club in the 1996/97 season; he dropped into non-league football. That night against the Belgium's would prove to be the highlight of his career.

–LEGENDS–

Jimmy Scoular

Jimmy Scoular was an ex-steel worker from Livingstone in Scotland. He made his name in the back four of Portsmouth's championship-winning side in 1949 and 1950. He also led Newcastle United to victory in the 1955 FA Cup final and picked up nine caps for Scotland. After hanging up his boots in 1964 he became manager of Bradford and, later that year, became boss at Ninian Park. Cardiff were in Division Two and were becoming an ageing side which meant Scoular had the unenviable task of getting rid of the older players at the club and giving youth a chance in the form of Phil Dwyer and John Toshack.

Jim's time at Ninian Park also corresponded with success in the Welsh Cup and that meant some fantastic games under the new floodlights at Ninian Park. Jimmy embraced European football and always said that "playing European teams would make Cardiff City players better". Although Scoular never had domestic success at the Bluebirds, he steadied a very rocky ship with his wheeling and dealing. He will always be remembered for those foreign outings in Europe, as well as his dour demeanour and booming Scots voice. Phil Dwyer, who played for Jimmy throughout Jimmy's Cardiff managerial career, recalled: "We used to train on the park across the road from Ninian Park and the park is surrounded by houses. It was a regular occurrence for the householders to come out and ask Jimmy to keep the swearing down as they could hear him in their front rooms. You could hear him screaming down the touchline. He was a real man's man." Jimmy left the Bluebirds in 1973 after a run of bad results and a boardroom takeover. He went to Newport County until he resigned in 1978. Jimmy died in 1998, aged 73.

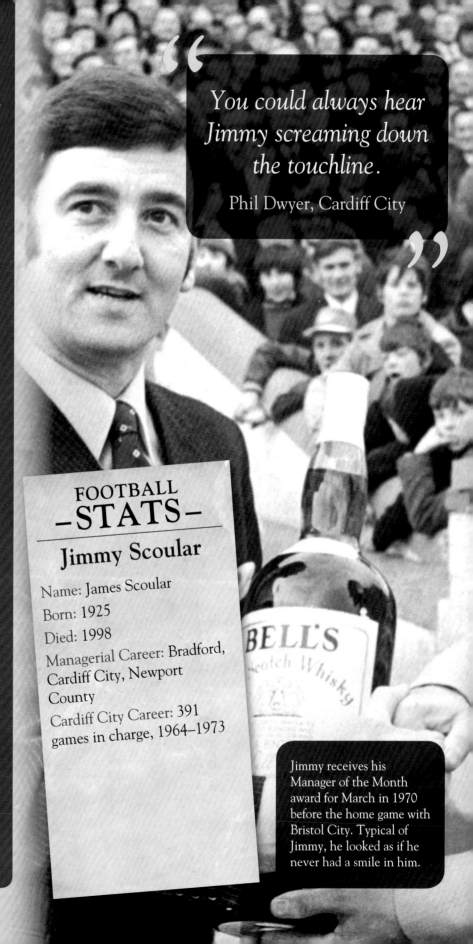

You could always hear Jimmy screaming down the touchline.

Phil Dwyer, Cardiff City

FOOTBALL –STATS–

Jimmy Scoular

Name: James Scoular

Born: 1925

Died: 1998

Managerial Career: Bradford, Cardiff City, Newport County

Cardiff City Career: 391 games in charge, 1964–1973

Jimmy receives his Manager of the Month award for March in 1970 before the home game with Bristol City. Typical of Jimmy, he looked as if he never had a smile in him.

RIGHT: After the sending off of Don Murray in the 1966 Welsh Cup final, Jimmy hides Don's face from the Press photographers.

BELOW: Jimmy with the Cardiff City players looking at their achievement in the *South Wales Echo* Real Madrid Special.

LEFT: In his playing days: Jimmy leads out Newcastle United in the 1955 FA Cup final against Manchester City – a game they would win 3-1.

RIGHT: A rare smile from Scoular as he shows the FA Cup to his wife at Newcastle United's winner's reception in 1955.

Brian tussles in the air with Charlton Athletic's Dave Shipperley during a game at Ninian Park in 1971.

–LEGENDS–

Brian Clark

Like Hughie Ferguson in the 1920s, Brian Clark will be remembered for scoring one of Cardiff City's most memorable goals. At a floodlit Ninian Park in March 1971, Brian rose into the air, as Cardiff fans waited with baited breath, and smashed the ball into the mighty Real Madrid's net to send the club and himself into the history books.

Brian's goalscoring pedigree was there for everyone to see. Son of Bristol City's striker and goalscoring record holder Don Clark, Brian started his footballing career at the Ashton Gate club in the shadow of his father. In his time at Bristol he forged a wonderful partnership with John Atyeo, which brought Brian 83 goals in a six-year spell, before he moved to Huddersfield Town in 1966.

Unable to settle up north Clark was picked up by Jimmy Scoular for £8,000. With Brian scoring two goals on his debut against Derby County, he became an instant hit with the Bluebird fans. The fans particularly loved his partnership with the young John Toshack. Clark continued scoring and became the club's leading scorer three seasons in a row.

Strangely allowed to leave the club in 1972, he went to Bournemouth, then later Millwall, and in 1975 Cardiff manager Jimmy Andrews brought him back on a free transfer where he helped the club to promotion and the Welsh Cup before ending his career at Newport County. Brian will always be remembered for THAT goal. But he should also be remembered as a model professional on and off the pitch. He was a true gentleman.

BELOW: Brian with Jimmy Scoular finishing off the particulars of his move to Cardiff City for £8,000 from Huddersfield Town. It would prove a steal when compared to what he contributed to the club. Apparently, the actual deal was done at the Severn Bridge Service Station outside Bristol at 7pm at night. Clark signed a blank contract and asked Scoular to fill the rest in later as he was so desperate to sign for the Bluebirds.

ABOVE: Brian's wife Gill unveils the sign honouring her late husband. The sign shows the way to the Capital Retail Park at the Cardiff City Stadium. The decision by Cardiff Council to honour Brian was made after consultation with Bluebird fans.

FOOTBALL
–STATS–
Brian Clark

Name: Brian Clark

Born: 1943

Died: 2010

Playing Career: Bristol City, Huddersfield Town, Cardiff City, Bournemouth, Millwall, Cardiff City, Newport County

Cardiff City Appearances: 267

Cardiff City Goals: 108

Clark with his trademark header in a match against Oxford United.

> *I would never have achieved what I did in the game without Brian Clark.*
>
> John Toshack speaking after the death of Brian Clark

–LEGENDS–

Don Murray

Don Murray was a man mountain in the heart of Cardiff City's defence. He made his debut aged 17 against Middlesbrough and, although the result went against Cardiff, those watching knew that this raw lad from the Highlands of Scotland was going to be around for a few years to say the least.

That rawness certainly got Murray into a few scrapes with the referees in the early days, but as maturity came so the big Scotsman got better. Don led Cardiff City by example at numerous European games and at times he seemed to take on attacks single-handed.

Rarely troubled by injury, he played 146 consecutive games for the Bluebirds, which is a record to this day. Don left Cardiff for his beloved Scotland in 1974 when he joined Edinburgh club Hearts, but he returned to his adopted Wales in 1976, joining his old boss Jimmy Scoular at Newport County, where he ended his career.

FOOTBALL –STATS–

Don Murray

Name: Donald Murray

Born: 1946

Playing Career: Cardiff City, Hearts, Newport County

Cardiff City Appearances: 532

Cardiff City Goals: 9

Mr 100%: Don Murray was one of the mainstays during Cardiff City's European adventures.

> *We knew not much would get past Don.*
>
> Brian Clark

LEFT: Don in typical captain pose rallying the troops in 1972.

The Seventies
1970-1979

The Cardiff City 1974/75 squad pictured with the Welsh Cup. Back row, left to right: Don Murray, Leighton Phillips, George Smith, Derek Showers, Bill Irwin, Freddie Pethard, Ron Healey, Jack Witham, Johnny Vincent, John Impey and Willie Anderson. Front row, left to right: John Farrington, Dave Powell, Phil Dwyer, Gil Reece, Jimmy Andrews (manager), Gary Bell, Richie Morgan, Tony Villars and Clive Charles.

1970 Cardiff City youth team lose a two-legged FA Youth Cup final to Arsenal. John Toshack signs for Liverpool in a £110,000 deal. **1971** The Bluebirds finish 19th in the league. **1972** Phil Dwyer makes his Cardiff City debut against Leyton Orient. **1973** Frank O'Farrell becomes manager for just 24 games. **1974** Cardiff are relegated to Division Three. **1975** Cardiff are promoted to Division Two. **1976** The club finish 18th in Division Two. Robin Friday signs from Reading for £28,000. **1977** Peter Sayer's goal knocks out Spurs in the FA Cup. **1978** Robin Friday has his contract terminated. **1979** 22,000 fans at Ninian Park see Cardiff draw 0-0 with Arsenal in the FA Cup.

The Seventies

The Seventies for Cardiff City were spent mainly in the second tier of English football, with the odd promotion and relegation thrown in for good measure. Success in the European Cup Winners' Cup vastly overshadowed anything the club had done in the league. But the decade did have its highpoints for the club including the emergence of Phil Dwyer, who would have his debut in 1972 and become Mr Cardiff City by the end of the decade. Although Cardiff fans love a local prospect coming through the ranks, they were equally angry at the loss of another local lad John Toshack who moved to Liverpool in 1970. Supporters felt that the club were on the brink of something good with Toshack and Clark leading the line but, unfortunately, like many Cardiff City directors before and after them, the board decided to take the money, which seemed to condemn the team to more years in the lower leagues.

With football's top flight littered with showmen like George Best, Rodney Marsh, Charlie George and Peter Osgood, the City fans, although in the Second Division, were desperate for their own iconic figure, and the 1970s brought one from along the M4 at Reading in the shape of Robin Friday. He would not stay long, but Cardiff City fans will forever remember that decade as the one they saw Friday play in.

–LEGENDS– Robin Friday

Robin Friday will always be somewhat of an enigma to Cardiff City fans. In an age where football was littered with entertainers, Cardiff certainly had their own down in South Wales. Friday started his career at non-league Hayes, and that part-time footballer mentality never left him; he always looked upon football as a bit of fun whilst concentrating on his trade of roofing. He kept this mentality throughout his professional career.

Friday was picked up by Reading where he scored 46 goals in 121 games. Cardiff manager Jimmy Andrews took a gamble and signed him for £28,000. On the day he was supposed to sign for the Bluebirds Andrews took a call from British Transport Police to say they had Friday in custody for fare dodging. Andrews had to go to Cardiff station to pick him up and take him to Ninian Park to sign his contract. Friday was a complete one-off and would arrive for training covered in roofing bitumen and with his boots in a carrier bag, and although the Cardiff fans loved having their very own "George Best", constant episodes involving discipline on and off the field, including several bouts of going missing, meant the club had no option but to cancel his contract after only 21 appearances.

Friday retired in 1977 and went back to the building trade, but in 1990 he was found dead in his basement flat in Acton, London after suffering a heart attack; he was 38 years old. Due to the lack of TV coverage for the lower leagues at the time there are few clips of Friday in action, which is a shame as he was an extraordinary footballer who may well have flourished in the modern game.

FOOTBALL –STATS–
Robin Friday

Name: Robin Friday
Born: 1952
Died: 1990
Playing career: Reading, Cardiff City
Cardiff City Appearances: 21
Cardiff City Goals: 6

" *Robin was so frustrating. One minute he would dribble past four players, and then he would punch the centre-half.* "

Jimmy Andrews,
Cardiff City manager

Robin Friday signs for Cardiff City from Reading. Here he is, with manager Jimmy Andrews, on the day of the signing. If only Jimmy knew what was to come!

ABOVE: Typical of Friday. Here he is in training for the FA Cup-tie against neighbours Bristol Rovers wearing his own T-shirt and sweatpants instead of a training kit.

LEFT: Robin ready for a game in the 1977 season.

This iconic picture now adorns thousands of modern-day Cardiff City fans' T-shirts and other memorabilia. Friday gives a two-fingered salute to Luton Town keeper Milija Aleksic after scoring his second goal at Ninian Park.

Friday being closely marked by Fulham defender John Lacey. Despite the close marking Friday would go on to score two goals in the game.

In trouble again. Friday receives a yellow card against Charlton Athletic. Later in the game he fractured his cheekbone.

LEFT: Friday lets the referee know what he thinks of his decision.

RIGHT: Friday, pictured on 15th April 1977, after leaving the Royal Hotel, Cardiff after appearing at a Football Association disciplinary hearing. This would typify Robin's career at the Bluebirds as it was his indiscipline on and off the field that ultimately led to his departure in 1978. He has become a terrace cult hero over the years for those very antics on and off the field, but we must also remember that when he was "on song" nobody could touch him. He was our very own 70s superstar.

ABOVE: Cardiff midfielder Ian Gibson in action against QPR in March 1971.

LEFT: John Toshack's replacement Alan Warboys in action on the opening day of the 1972 season against Luton Town; Cardiff won 2-1. Warboys was signed in 1970 from Sheffield Wednesday for a then record fee of £42,000. He filled Toshack's boots admirably, scoring 27 goals in 56 games, and left in 1972 as part of a deal with Sheffield United that brought Gil Reece and Dave Powell to Ninian Park.

1972–75

ABOVE: Richie Morgan pictured during a game with team-mate Albert Lamour watching. Morgan would manage the Bluebirds from 1978–1981.

ABOVE: Cardiff's Willie Anderson chases after the ball along with Bolton Wanderers' Mike Walsh at Ninian Park.

Wales international Mike England chases a ball in a Cardiff game against Exeter City in 1975. England joined Cardiff from Tottenham Hotspur and his experience was a major factor in Cardiff's promotion in 1975. England would go on to manage the Welsh national team in the 1980s.

Perhaps the football on show throughout the Seventies was not that sparkling at Ninian Park. This fan in the Canton Stand certainly thinks so as he sleeps through the game to the amusement of the rest of the crowd.

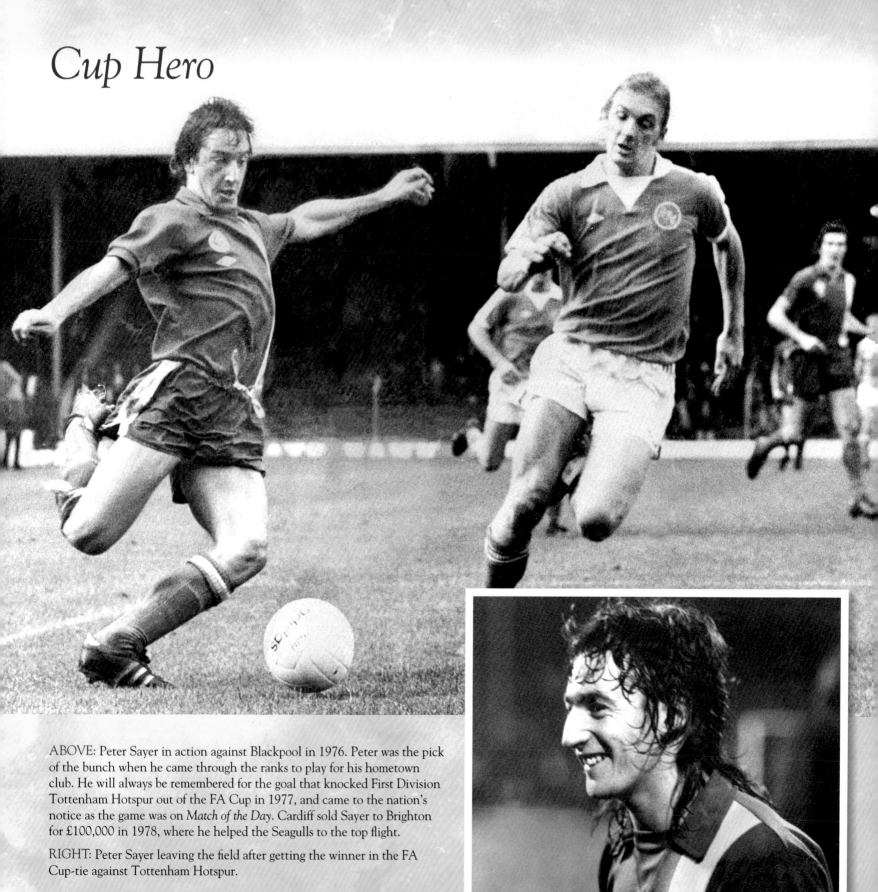

Cup Hero

ABOVE: Peter Sayer in action against Blackpool in 1976. Peter was the pick of the bunch when he came through the ranks to play for his hometown club. He will always be remembered for the goal that knocked First Division Tottenham Hotspur out of the FA Cup in 1977, and came to the nation's notice as the game was on *Match of the Day*. Cardiff sold Sayer to Brighton for £100,000 in 1978, where he helped the Seagulls to the top flight.

RIGHT: Peter Sayer leaving the field after getting the winner in the FA Cup-tie against Tottenham Hotspur.

Manager Jimmy Andrews with goalscorer Tony Villars after his goal in a 1-1 draw against Crystal Palace secured Second Division status for the Bluebirds in 1975 in front of 26,000 fans at Ninian Park.

The Great Escape

ABOVE: John Buchanan celebrates a goal, along with team-mate Keith Pontin, against Leyton Orient.

RIGHT: Derek Showers takes the applause from the Canton Stand after scoring against Nottingham Forest in 1974.

Cardiff City's 1978 squad who finished ninth in Division Two. Back row, left to right: Gary Harris, Alan Campbell, Paul Went, Keith Pontin, John Davies, Ron Healey, John Buchanan, Freddie Pethard, Steve Grapes and Tony Beasley. Front row, left to right: Phil Leach, Gerry Byrne, Rod Thomas, Brian Attley, Phil Dwyer, Jimmy Andrews (manager), Richie Morgan, Ray Bishop, Tony Evans, David Giles and Anton Joseph.

115

–LEGENDS–

Phil Dwyer

Phil Dwyer's appearance record for Cardiff City I am sure will never be beaten, particularly in an age where the modern footballer stays around 18 months at a club before they "need a new challenge". Dwyer's love affair with Cardiff City started in the 1960s when he joined the groundstaff. He was part of the Cardiff FA Youth Cup final side of 1970 that lost to Arsenal, and it was not long before manager Jimmy Scoular threw him in for his debut against Leyton Orient in 1972.

It proved a masterstroke, as Dwyer kept his place and seemed to revel in the step-up to the first team. Part of the promotion side of 1975, Dwyer also gained 10 caps for Wales, playing a few games as striker. Although he has a hardman reputation Phil is respected throughout the game and loved by the Cardiff City fans for giving 100% in every game; they always looked upon him as "one of their own". Although Dwyer was in and out of the treatment room at times, it was a shock to everyone when manager Alan Durban sold him to Rochdale in 1985 and thus closed the door on one of the club's greats. Typical of Phil, he almost single-handedly kept Rochdale in the league with some dogged displays in the heart of defence and, although they wanted him to extend his contract, he came back to Wales and retired from the game.

Trademark Dwyer as Phil puts the Bluebirds 1-0 up against Nottingham Forest in a 2-1 win.

FOOTBALL –STATS–

Phil Dwyer

Name: Philip Dwyer

Born: 1953

Playing Career: Cardiff City, Rochdale, Wales

Cardiff City Appearances: 575

Cardiff City Goals: 41

Wales Appearances: 10

Wales Goals: 2

> *On and off the pitch he was the life and soul of the club.*
>
> Len Ashurst, Cardiff City manager

Relaxing after training. Phil Dwyer leaning on the dugout at Ninian Park.

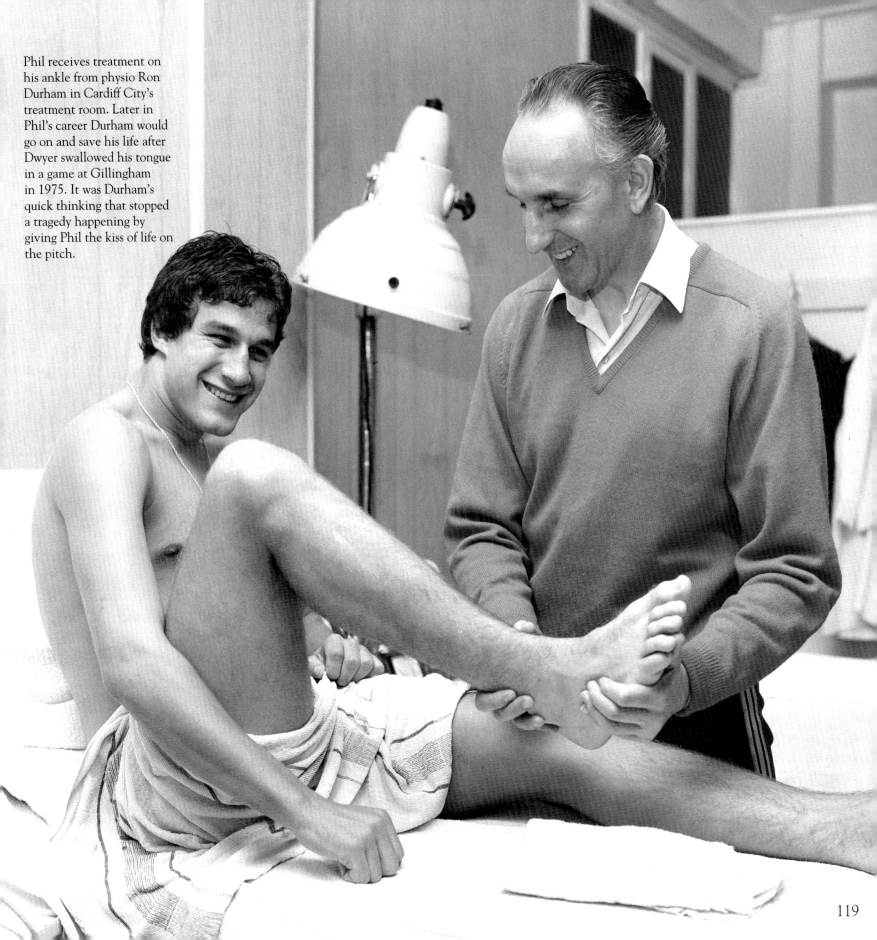

Phil receives treatment on his ankle from physio Ron Durham in Cardiff City's treatment room. Later in Phil's career Durham would go on and save his life after Dwyer swallowed his tongue in a game at Gillingham in 1975. It was Durham's quick thinking that stopped a tragedy happening by giving Phil the kiss of life on the pitch.

When FOOTBALL Was FOOTBALL

Shoots of Recovery
1980-2000

Cardiff City players
celebrate promotion
in 1988 after the
game against Crewe
Alexandra. Back row,
left to right: Brian
McDermott, Mike Ford,
Nicky Platnauer, Nigel
Stevenson, George
Wood, Phil Bater and
Paul Wheeler. Front
row, left to right:
Steve Mardenborough,
Mark Kelly and
Kevin Bartlett.

1981 Cardiff City are relegated to Division Three. 1982 Cardiff are promoted to Division Two. 1983 Manager Len Ashurst resigns. 1984 Phil Dwyer breaks Tom Farquharson's appearance record. 1985 The club are relegated to Division Three. 1986 The Bluebirds are relegated to Division Four. Frank Burrows becomes manager. 1987 Jason Perry makes his debut. 1988 Cardiff are promoted to Division Three. 1989 Yet another relegation – Cardiff are back down to Division Four and Frank Burrows leaves. 1990 Cardiff sit in Division Four. 1991 Eddie May becomes manager. 1992/93 Cardiff win promotion and the Welsh Cup. 1993 Cardiff appear back in Europe getting knocked out of the European Cup Winners' Cup by Standard Liege in the first round. 1994 The Bluebirds are relegated again. One highlight – Cardiff knock Manchester City out of the FA Cup. 1995 Cardiff finish 22nd and are safe from re-election. 1996 Cardiff reach the play-offs but are knocked out by Northampton Town. 1998 Frank Burrows becomes manager for the second time. Cardiff win promotion to Division Two. 1999/2000 Burrows leaves his post and Cardiff are relegated yet again.

The Eighties (Down in the Basement)

The 1980s will always be remembered as a decade of excess: Champagne, Yuppies and loadsamoney. Nothing could have been more further from the truth at Ninian Park at that time. It really was life in the basement for the club. Inconsistency was what the club were all about. The decade produced seven managerial casualties, four relegations and two promotions. It really is safe to say that every fan experienced every kind of emotion in that time. Football itself, nationally, was at an all-time low with the Hillsborough tragedy and Heysel Stadium disaster being a real watershed for the game. The fences that had penned supporters throughout the Seventies were being torn down by clubs after they were thought to be a contributing factor to making the grounds unsafe. For Cardiff City the decade started with relegation and ended with one, and with no money in the club and attendances at an all-time low, it became a labour of love for every watching Bluebird fan.

LEFT: Empty terraces but a few fans in the trees behind the Grangetown End as Cardiff entertain QPR in 1982.

Cardiff City's Alan Curtis was chaired off the field after Cardiff's game against Crewe Alexandra secured promotion in 1988. Curtis, a legend in Welsh football, joined the Bluebirds in 1986 on a free transfer and would go on to play 125 games for the Bluebirds and score 10 goals. He left for Swansea City in 1989. Curtis was one of the few players who played for both South Wales' clubs and still has the respect of both sets of fans today.

Ex-England midfielder Gerry Francis joins the club in 1984. Francis made little improvement, despite his obvious talent, and left after a season to join Portsmouth. Here he is on the day he signed, with manager Jimmy Goodfellow (left) and managing director Ron Jones.

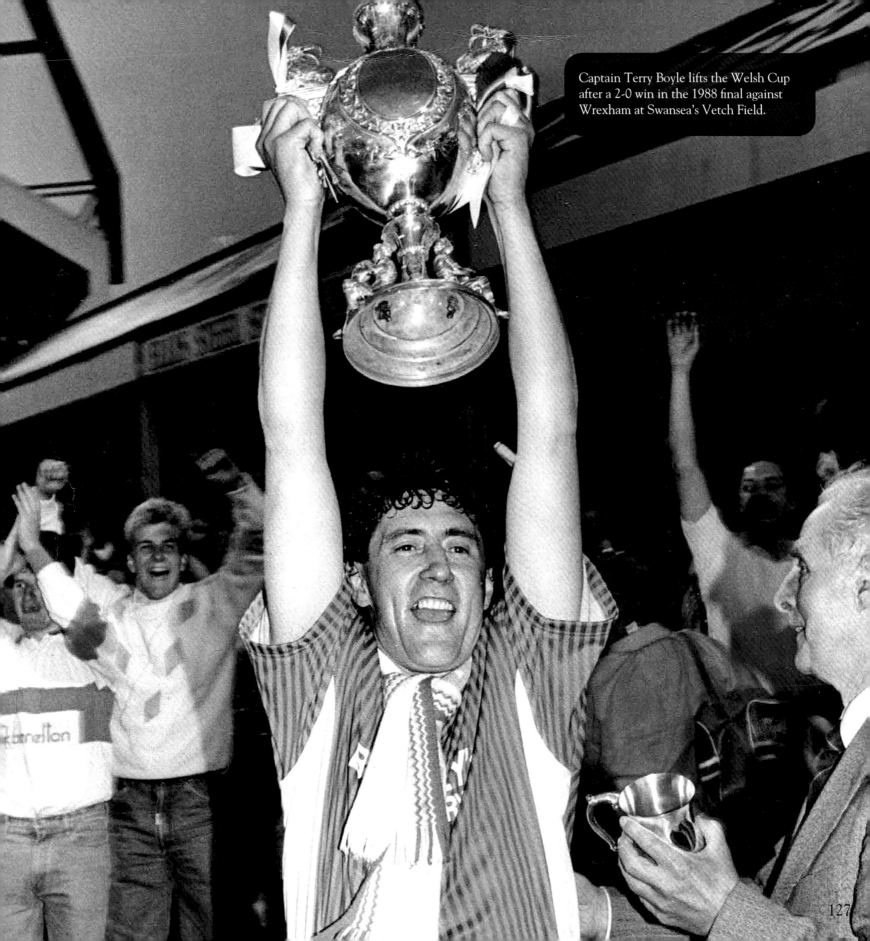

Captain Terry Boyle lifts the Welsh Cup after a 2-0 win in the 1988 final against Wrexham at Swansea's Vetch Field.

Roger celebrates a goal with striker Chris Pike.

–LEGENDS–

Roger Gibbins

When Roger Gibbins arrived on a free transfer from Cambridge United in 1982 it would prove to be one of manager Len Ashurst's best ever deals. Gibbins had certainly been here and there before coming to Ninian Park but that experience would prove invaluable to the club at that time.

He went on to be an ever-present in the side as the club won promotion. He left for rivals Swansea City, as a result of Cardiff City having no money, and finished his playing career at Newport County until his retirement in 1991.

Roger then returned to Cardiff City as manager Eddie May's assistant, where they clinched another promotion for the club.

FOOTBALL –STATS–

Roger Gibbins

Name: Roger Gibbins

Born: 1955

Playing Career: Spurs, Oxford United, Norwich City, New England Tea Men, Cambridge United, Cardiff City, Swansea City, Newport County

Cardiff City Appearances: 345

Cardiff City Goals: 33

Roger controlling the play again.

The Nineties (On the Up)

"The only way is up" was a popular saying around the terraces as Cardiff City started the 1990s. They found themselves in the Fourth Division of English football and by the start of the new millennium the club would be unrecognizable. An incredible nine managers would be in charge of the club through the decade and not one of them had a bean to spend on anything, wheeling and dealing to keep the club afloat. But the club were on the up and to the hardcore terrace faithful that was all they could ask for. A light at the end of a very long tunnel.

Cardiff City's 1993 promotion winning squad. Back row, left to right: Rick Wright (chairman), Lee Baddeley, Gavin Ward, Chris Pike, Nicky Richardson, Jason Perry, Roger Gibbins, Derek Brazil, Nathan Blake, Mark Grew, Paul Miller, Harry Parsons (kit man) and Jimmy Goodfellow (physio). Front row, left to right: Phil Stant, Cohen Griffith, Damon Searle, Paul Ramsey, Robbie James, Carl Dale and Eddie May (manager).

Captain Paul Ramsey is crowned by his team-mates as Cardiff beat Rhyl 5-0 at the National Stadium in Cardiff to win the 1993 Welsh Cup and another passport to Europe.

Cardiff City striker Nathan Blake is carried off the Ninian Park pitch by Bluebird supporters after beating Shrewsbury Town 2-1 in front of 17,000 fans and securing the 1993 Division Three title.

–LEGENDS–

Phil Stant

"Ooh aah Stantona" would be the call from the Cardiff City fans as this old-school centre-forward would run out to give his all for the Bluebirds. Phil Stant was just like the centre-forwards of old: big, strong and brave.

A veteran of the Falklands War, Stant was truly loved by the Cardiff City fans. With his big forearms on show, his tattoos stuck out as his trademark – not tattoos like the ones that footballers have today, these tattoos were the result of being in the Army and looked like the type your Granddad would have.

Stant started his career at Hereford United, who bought him out of the Army, and after various moves around the lower leagues he was signed by Cardiff City for £100,000 from Mansfield in 1992 and thus started his cult status at the club.

Stant was the perfect target man for Eddie May's side and Stant and Carl Dale got their share of the goals. Unfortunately Stant joined Bury in 1995 after contract problems with the then Cardiff City owner Rick Wright. Stant left Bury and went to Brighton, where he retired from league football soon after. He was truly a working-class hero for a working-class club and that's why they loved him.

FOOTBALL –STATS–

Phil Stant

Name: Philip Stant

Born: 1962

Playing Career: Hereford United, Notts County, Fulham, Mansfield, Cardiff City, Bury, Brighton

Cardiff City Appearances: 106

Cardiff City Goals: 55

LEFT: "He's tough, he's mean, he fought the Argentine."

BELOW: Stant goes for goal against Cambridge United in 1994.

–LEGENDS–

Eddie May

When Eddie May took the manager's job in 1991, Cardiff City were in Division Four and the club needed a lift. May produced an exciting and, more importantly for the time, successful side that won the league title the following year. His spell at the club gave supporters a real lift and the club looked to be going in one direction and that was very much upwards. Unfortunately for May finances kicked in and the cash-strapped club sacked May in 1994 when a new consortium took over.

He returned for only eight games in 1995, following the collapse of a takeover, but left when his services were no longer needed. Eddie May will always have a place in Cardiff City's heart if only for giving them one of the best seasons they had in a long time – the season of 1993. Eddie passed away in April 2012 and his ashes have been scattered in a Garden of Remembrance at the club's stadium.

FOOTBALL –STATS–

Eddie May

Name: Edwin May

Born: 1943

Died: 2012

Managerial History at Cardiff City: Games 148 matches (first spell) 1991–1994; 8 Matches (second spell) 1995

> *Eddie would just give you a look.*
>
> Jason Perry

Eddie May, with owner Rick Wright, celebrating promotion gained at Wrexham's Racecourse ground in 1993.

–LEGENDS–

Carl Dale

Carl Dale learnt his trade in the tough Welsh league. Although at Arsenal as a youngster he never made the grade but, instead of giving up, he played for Rhyl, Colwyn Bay and Bangor City, and it was there that he was picked up by Chester City where he scored 41 goals in 116 games.

Signed by manager Eddie May in 1991 for £100,000, Dale formed a prolific partnership with Chris Pike upfront leading Cardiff's promotion winning side. Although plagued by injury the Bluebird fans loved him as he always seemed to be in the right place at the right time. He left Cardiff City in 1998 and joined Yeovil Town and Newport County, where he continued to score goals, before retiring.

FOOTBALL –STATS–

Carl Dale

Name: Carl Dale

Born: 1966

Playing career: Chester City, Cardiff City, Yeovil Town, Newport County

Cardiff City Appearances: 274

Cardiff City Goals: 108

Carl under pressure from a Plymouth Argyle player.

–LEGENDS–

Jason Perry

Jason Perry made his debut against Exeter City in the 1987 season. Perry came through the ranks at City and nobody loves a local lad making the grade more than the City faithful. His tough-tackling, mature approach made him seem a lot older than he was. A part of Eddie May's promotion winning side, Perry established himself in the Bluebird's line-up and only injury could force him out. A serious injury did hinder him in the 1995 season but Perry, being the man he is, fought back to take his place in the Cardiff line-up once again. And when the crowd cheered the first tackle he made on his return it was like he had never been away.

It was a major shock to all fans when he was given a free transfer to Bristol Rovers, and it turned out to be Rovers' gain and City's loss as he put in performance after performance for the Pirates. Moves to Lincoln City and Hull City followed before a spell at Newport County, after which he hung up his boots. Perry gave 100% in every game that he played for Cardiff City, and supporters will remember him for a long time to come.

Perry determined as ever.

FOOTBALL –STATS–

Jason Perry

Name: Jason Perry

Born: 1970

Playing Career: Cardiff City, Bristol Rovers, Lincoln City, Hull City, Newport County, Wales

Cardiff City Appearances: 361

Cardiff City Goals: 5

Wales Appearances: 1

Wales Goals: 0

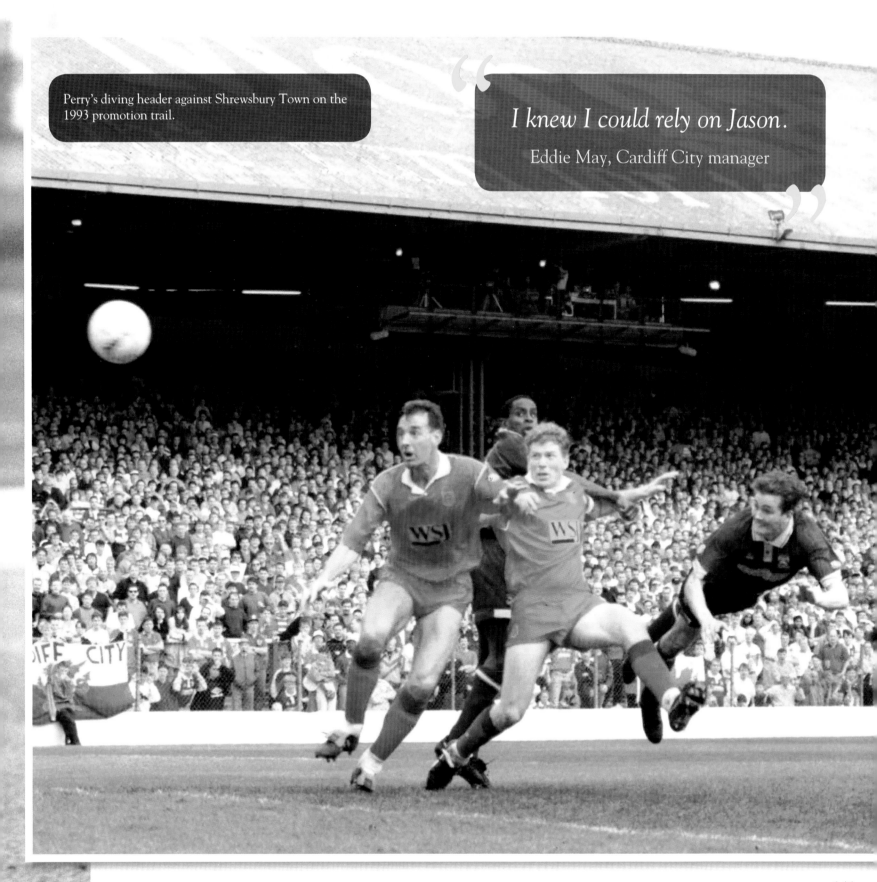

Perry's diving header against Shrewsbury Town on the 1993 promotion trail.

I knew I could rely on Jason.

Eddie May, Cardiff City manager

Scorer Kevin Nugent (left) celebrates his goal against Brighton at Ninian Park, with Scott Young (middle) and Wayne O'Sullivan, in the club's 1998 promotion season. The team would go on and finish third in the league, securing a place in Division Two.

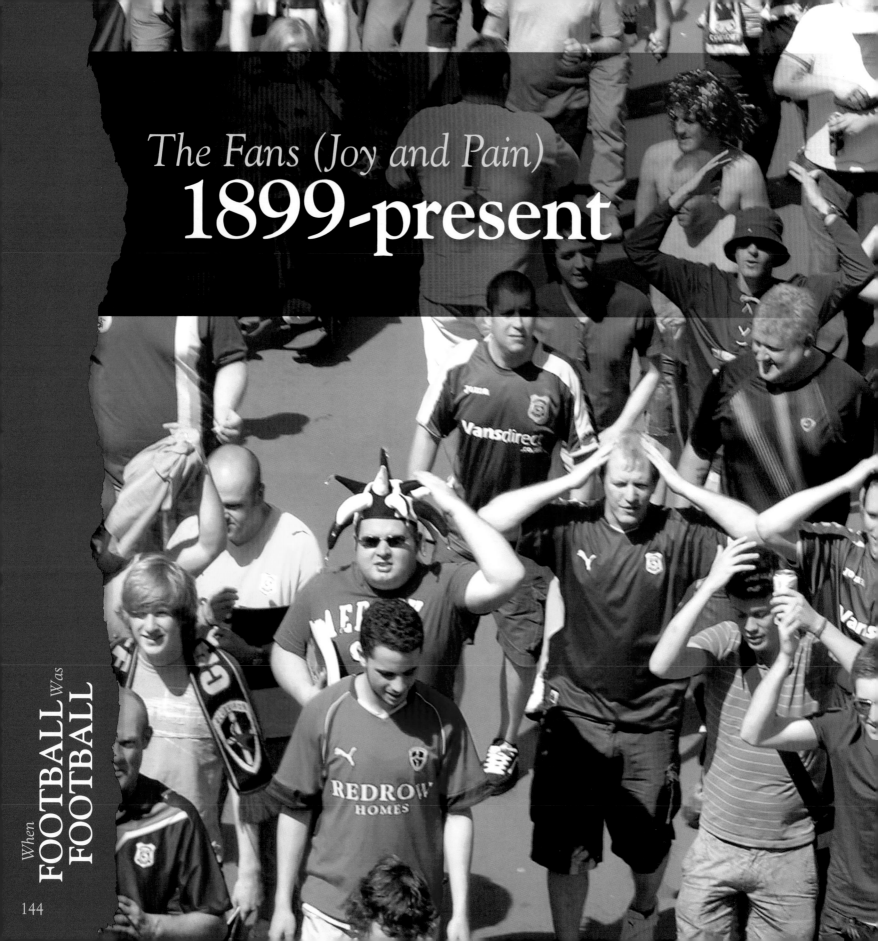

The Fans (Joy and Pain)
1899-present

"Do the Ayatollah", "Do the Ayatollah"

In 1990 around 150 Cardiff City fans stood on the away terrace at Sincil Bank, home of Lincoln City, and the Ayatollah was born. Riot police turned up complete with a police surveillance camera crew. It was obvious that the local constabulary were expecting trouble from their visitors from South Wales, who were fed up of watching a dire 0-0 draw.

The police vastly outnumbered the Bluebird fans. One fan started to run around the terrace tapping his head on both sides and with that all the other fans joined in.

The practice of tapping your head was linked to the Iranians in the 1980s who showed it as a display of pain and anguish. It was particularly evident during their leader Ayatollah Khomeini's funeral where thousands of mourners did it to show their distress at his passing. This obviously struck a chord with the Cardiff fans who had been subjected to many a painful display by their team over the years.

The practice is done to this day by Bluebird fans and players alike as a sign of celebration and support for the team, and it has even crept into other sports, with rugby player Gareth Thomas and athlete Dai Green doing it in various events.

ABOVE: Cardiff's former striker Michael Chopra "Does the Ayatollah" on joining the club.

Cardiff City fans queue to get in the ground in 1957.

Five young lads look over the enclosure wall for a better view in 1961.

After the recent instalment of floodlights at Ninian Park many fans used them to get a better view if they couldn't get a ticket.

Every emotion watching the Bluebirds.

ABOVE: Cardiff City supporters getting ready for another trip to Wembley.

BELOW: Supporter Dave Allen, with his two grandchildren Maddie and Cian, outside his decorated house.

Despair at a play-off defeat.

ABOVE: The joy of a goal at Wembley!

LEFT: Tributes laid at the Ninian Park gates in memory of Cardiff City fan Mike Dye who died at Wembley Stadium ahead of the England v Wales 2011 Euro qualifier. A perfect example of how the fans come together.

Cardiff fans Joseph Turner and Tom Evans at the last fixture at Ninian Park.

159

The Men in the Boardroom
1899-present

The boardroom at Cardiff City has never been a place for the faint hearted. Every chairman who has run the club I'm sure has done it with the best intentions, but whether it's a local businessman or a multi-million-pound international investor, it has always been a famine or feast existence for the fans.

LEFT: Cardiff City board members, left to right: Dr Alex Brownlea, Walter Riden, Herbert Merrett (chairman), Chris Page and Tudor Street outside the Ninian Park offices in the 1946/47 season. At the time, the board were criticized for spending £9,000 on ground improvements to Ninian Park instead of spending it on the team.

ABOVE: Sir Herbert Merrett addresses the crowd following the team's return to Division One in 1952. Merrett was a coal merchant who joined the board in the 1930s and was at the club for over 25 years. He became a Sir in 1950 for services to public life.

1910 S H Nicholls becomes the club's first chairman. **1919** With the club in the black the board sanction ground improvements. **1925** The directors invest in an electric mower and roller, which means the groundsman has to sell the club horse. **1927** The general strike affects attendances as they drop by a third. **1932** A sporting carnival is organized to help the club's finances. **1933** The board goes to the FA to seek re-election. The club have a £1,000 tax bill and a police bill for £173. **1939** Coal exporter Herbert Merrett becomes chairman. **1946** The board announce they are £18,000 in the black. **1947** The board spend £9,000 on ground improvements. **1950** Herbert Merrett is knighted for services to the public. **1958** Merrett resigns from the board. **1959** Local businessman Ron Beecher becomes chairman. **1962** Local shipping boss Fred Deeney becomes chairman. **1972** David Goldstone becomes chairman. **1977** The board turn down former player John Toshack's offer to become player-manager. **1983** The club's overall debt is £1.4 million. **1986** Local businessman Tony Clemo takes over the reins. **1991** Barry Island theme park owner Rick Wright buys the club. **1992** Wright takes out an insurance policy on the club getting promotion, which they did, and it pays out £1.4 million to Wright. **1993** Wright tries to sell the club. **1995** Birmingham businessman Samesh Kumar buys the club for £850,000. **2000** Sam Hammam buys the club for £3 million. **2001** The board pay a record £1 million for Graham Kavanagh from Stoke City. **2003** The club sets up an academy to source local young talent. **2005** Hammam invites Peter Ridsdale to join the board. **2006** Ridsdale gains control of the club. **2009** HMRC issues a winding-up order on the club for an unpaid £1.9 million tax bill. **2010** Ridsdale leaves as a Malaysian consortium buys the club.

Cardiff City manager Jimmy Scoular (far right) sat with Cardiff City directors in the boardroom at Ninian Park, 1964.

David Watkins (left) of the Rugby Football League and director Bob Grogan at the launch of "Bringing Rugby League to Cardiff". Grogan's engineering company, Kenton Utilities, owned the club, and the northeast businessman was a big rugby league fan. The venture never really got off the ground. Grogan passed away in 1984.

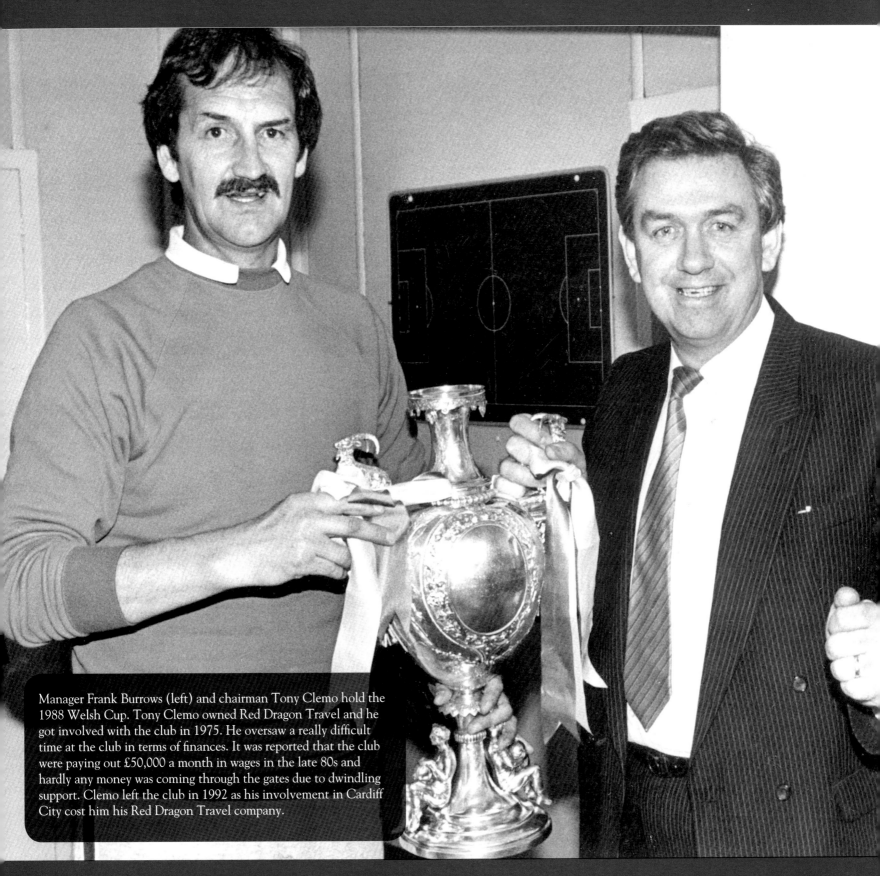

Manager Frank Burrows (left) and chairman Tony Clemo hold the 1988 Welsh Cup. Tony Clemo owned Red Dragon Travel and he got involved with the club in 1975. He oversaw a really difficult time at the club in terms of finances. It was reported that the club were paying out £50,000 a month in wages in the late 80s and hardly any money was coming through the gates due to dwindling support. Clemo left the club in 1992 as his involvement in Cardiff City cost him his Red Dragon Travel company.

LEFT: Cardiff City chairman Rick Wright waves to the fans from the director's box at Ninian Park. Wright joined the club in 1991. He was a former Army frogman and commercial diver who owned the Barry Island theme park. When he joined the club he wiped out the debt and put the club on an even keel although he did state that he would only be involved for a few years. He brought an immediate enthusiasm and professional attitude to the club and this coincided with the club's 1993 promotion under manager Eddie May.

ABOVE: Wright left the Bluebirds in 1995, selling his shares to Birmingham businessman Samesh Kumar for £850,000. He left South Wales and went to live in Australia.

Lebanese businessman Sam Hammam became the owner of Cardiff City in 2000 after paying £3 million for the club. Hammam, ever the publicist, decided to change the club badge using the flag of St David, and he pledged to get the entire Welsh nation supporting the "Cardiff Celts", as would be the club's new name. The team would also sport a new kit of green, red and white. Thankfully this never happened. To his credit Hammam set the wheels in motion for a new stadium and also got the football community talking about the club for the right reasons. He was a man who realized the club's potential. Sam left the club in 2005.

ABOVE: Feeling the pressure.

RIGHT: Peter Ridsdale joined the board of Cardiff City in 2005 on the invitation of Sam Hammam, with a remit to oversee the new stadium project. When Hammam left, Ridsdale became chairman and, although not popular with some supporters due to his mismanagement of previous club Leeds United, he oversaw a successful time for the club, with an FA Cup final appearance and play-off final. But financial trouble was like a cloud hanging over the club and it reached a peak in 2009 when HMRC issued a winding-up order on the club for non-payment of taxes. The club worked out a deal with the High Court. It was quoted that the figure owed was as much as £1.9 million. Ridsdale left under a cloud in 2010 when a Malaysian consortium bought the club.

A new regime and a new era. Cardiff City's new Malaysian owner is Dato Chan Tien Ghee, or TG as he is known to the fans. Since the takeover by the Malaysian consortium the club have become more stable and have also established a Cardiff City academy in Malaysia in the hope of promoting the club in the lucrative Far East Market. They have started revolutionary plans for the club in the 2012/13 season by changing the kit from blue to red – the national colour of Malaysia, and in their opinion more dynamic for the Asian Market as well as being more relevant to Wales.

The owners also want to "bring together a fusion of cultures" by replacing the Bluebird on the club's badge with a dragon, again an important symbol in Malaysian culture. The future of Cardiff City is certainly going to be a very eventful one.

Into the Millennium
2000-present

As Cardiff City approached the new Millennium, the changing face of football could not have been more evident. Talk of a new stadium on the horizon and the introduction of an academy, which would go on and produce local lads that would become Cardiff stars of the future, were the way the club were moving. It was a time where the money paid to the modern players would seem incredible to the players of yesteryear, and with the new stadium a reality at the end of the decade, combined with visits to Wembley for the FA Cup final in 2008 and the League Cup final in 2012, it can't be long before the Bluebirds find themselves at football's top table.

Young clears away the danger.

2000 Bobby Gould takes over as boss. 2001 The Bluebirds are promoted to Division Two. 2002 Cardiff knock Premiership team Leeds United out of the FA Cup, 2-1. 2003 Robert Earnshaw breaks Stan Richards' goalscoring record. Cardiff win the play-off final at the Millennium Stadium 1-0 against QPR and are promoted to the Championship. 2004 City finish 16th in the Championship. 2005 Dave Jones is appointed manager. 2006 Michael Chopra signs from Newcastle United for £500,000. 2007 Cardiff finish the season 12th. 2008 The Bluebirds get to the FA Cup final losing 1-0 to Portsmouth. 2009 Cardiff lose the play-off final 3-2 to Blackpool. 2010 The Bluebirds lose the play-off semi-final to Reading, and Dave Jones leaves the club. 2011 The new manager, Malky Mackay, takes the club to the League Cup final at Wembley, where they lose on penalties to Liverpool. 2012 Cardiff City lose the Championship semi-final play-off to West Ham United over two legs.

Scott on the ball against Wolverhampton Wanderers in 1998.

–LEGENDS–

Scott Young

Scott Young will always be remembered for the goal that knocked out Premiership leaders Leeds United in the FA Cup in 2002. Even without that goal Youngy had a special place in the Cardiff City fans' hearts. Scott had that connection with the fans; they all knew that he was one of them and if he had not made it as a player he would be watching his beloved Bluebirds from the terraces and having a pint with other fans after.

Rising through the youth team ranks, Young made his debut, aged just 16 years old, in a 3-1 win against Stockport County. Scott was a tough no-nonsense defender who would have run through a brick wall to lead Cardiff to victory – who will ever forget how he got sent off for two bookable offences against rivals Swansea City after only being on the pitch for 10 minutes in 1997, such was his desire to beat them. Tragedy struck Scott when injury after injury forced him to retire aged just 28. After a failed comeback with Newport County, Cardiff City offered Young a job as community officer where he still is to this day.

FOOTBALL –STATS–

Scott Young

Name: Scott Young

Born: 1976

Playing Career: Cardiff City, Newport County

Cardiff City Appearances: 327

Cardiff City Goals: 26

–LEGENDS–

Rob Earnshaw

Rob Earnshaw was a product of the YTS system at Cardiff City. He came through the ranks to earn his first professional contract in 1998, and celebrated it by scoring against Hartlepool on the opening day of the season. After that tremendous start he was moved out on loan by manager Frank Burrows to get "Ernie" some valued experience, which seemed to work for the youngster.

Ernie won a regular place in the side and came of age in the 2002/03 season when he scored 31 goals, beating Stan Richards' record that had stood since 1947. Ernie was an instant hit with the fans particularly as he would always provide them with his trademark somersault goal celebration. In 2004 Cardiff City were suffering financial problems and their main asset was Ernie so, unfortunately for the fans, he was sold to WBA for £3 million.

Trips through the leagues with various clubs including Norwich City, Derby County and Nottingham Forest, led this terrace hero back to a very different Cardiff City from the one he had left. To the supporters Ernie is well respected; he has always played the game with a smile on his face. And let's not forget that somersault!

FOOTBALL
–STATS–

Rob Earnshaw

Name: Robert Earnshaw

Born: 1981

Playing Career: Cardiff City, WBA, Norwich City, Derby County, Nottingham Forest, Cardiff City, Wales

Cardiff City Appearances: 205

Cardiff City Goals: 105

Wales Appearances: 58

Wales Goals: 16

ABOVE: Ernie heads for goal in 2001; he is the only player ever to score hat-tricks in all football leagues, the FA Cup, the League Cup and in international football.

LEFT: Ernie gets ready for the trademark somersault after scoring against Mansfield Town in 2000.

Cardiff City manager Malky Mackay taking a training session. Mackay joined the club in 2010 after a playing career with Queens Park, Celtic, Norwich City, West Ham and Watford. It was at Watford that he became manager before joining the Bluebirds. Mackay has proved to be a big hit with the Bluebird faithful, taking the club to the Championship play-off semi-final and the League Cup final in his first year in charge.

ABOVE: Some of the Cardiff City squad training at the Vale of Glamorgan Training Complex.

BELOW: The future of the club: Cardiff City's Darcy Blake and Joe Ralls chatting outside Cardiff City's academy.

BELOW RIGHT: Modern-day training techniques. I wonder what the lads of 1927 would make of it?

ABOVE: Cardiff's next generation of youngsters, hoping to catch the manager's eye, at the academy.

LEFT: A product of the academy, midfielder Aaron Ramsey, captain of Wales, in action against England. Ramsey was brought through the academy and was later sold to Arsenal for £4.8 million in 2008.

–LEGENDS–

Michael Chopra

Everybody loves a goalscorer and Michael Chopra was certainly that. He joined the club from Newcastle United in 2006 for £500,000 and in his first season that price tag seemed a bargain as he netted 22 goals. Cardiff, as usual, cashed in on their star striker in 2007 when he was sold to Sunderland for £5 million. Chopra then returned to the Bluebirds in 2008 in a £3 million deal. In his time at the club "Chops" scored some important goals in big games like the play-off final against Blackpool where he opened the scoring after eight minutes. And he scored the winner against Swansea City in the 2010 Derby game, although many feel he went stale at the end of his time at Cardiff City, which prompted a move to Ipswich Town in 2011. Chops will always be remembered with fondness for those big game goals, which proved he was a big-time player and a Cardiff City favourite.

FOOTBALL STATS

Michael Chopra

Name: Michael Chopra

Born: 1983

Playing Career: Newcastle United, Cardiff City, Sunderland, Cardiff City, Ipswich Town

Cardiff City Appearances: 118

Cardiff City Goals: 52

Chopra scores the first goal in the 2009/10 play-off final against Blackpool.

Cardiff City full-back Kevin McNaughton sits alone and is inconsolable after Cardiff's 1-0 FA Cup final defeat to Portsmouth in 2008.

Another product of the academy: Joe Ledley scores for his hometown club against Blackpool in the play-off final. The game would be Ledley's last game for the club as he moved to Celtic in the close season.

ABOVE: Cardiff's Roger Johnson in an aerial battle in the 2008 FA Cup final against Portsmouth.

LEFT: Cardiff City shock the football world as they sign Manchester City striker Craig Bellamy on loan for the 2010/11 season. Bellamy is a Cardiff lad and his dream was always to play for his hometown club at some stage in his career. The deal brought comparisons to the John Charles deal way back in the 1960s when he signed from Roma.

BELOW: Manager Malky Mackay acknowledges the supporters after the heartbreaking League Cup defeat to Liverpool on penalties.

—LEGENDS—

Peter Whittingham

When Peter Whittingham arrived from Aston Villa, many Cardiff City fans thought "Oh well, another midfielder". How wrong they were. Granted, it didn't look good for the lad from Nuneaton at first – here he was joining the Bluebirds after not being able to gain a regular place in the Aston Villa team, and to look at him he was not what you would call an imposing figure for rival midfielders. But his vision for the killer pass and his outstanding ability to strike a dead ball with power from any angle, more than made up for any concerns about his build. Whittingham has never failed to give 100% to the Bluebirds' cause and, although bigger clubs from the Premiership have come calling, he has stayed loyal to the club, and in this day and age that is a rare commodity in any player and something the Bluebird fans will always remember.

FOOTBALL —STATS—

Peter Whittingham

Name: Peter Whittingham

Born: 1984

Playing Career: Aston Villa, Cardiff City

Cardiff City Appearances: 217

Cardiff City Goals: 54

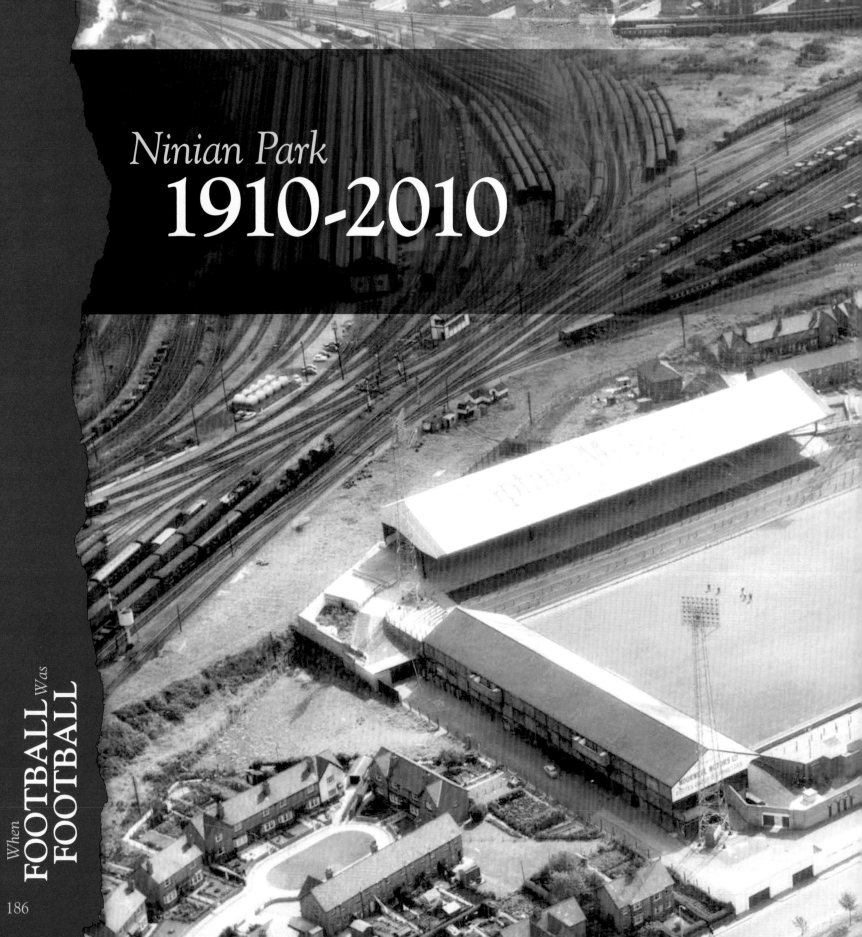

Ninian Park
1910-2010

Cardiff City's Ninian Park was like the 12ᵗʰ man to every Bluebirds side throughout the years. It was tight, compact and to any visiting side it could also be very intimidating. Over the years it has seen everything, from the FA Cup housed in its trophy cabinet, to the mighty Real Madrid side running out of its tunnel, to Pope John Paul II saying prayers in front of 58,000 on its pitch. Built on an ash mound in the Leckwith area of Cardiff in the 1900s, it has served the Bluebirds well. But as football has changed over the years clubs have to cater for different things such as easy parking, corporate hospitality, restaurants and even retail shopping outlets within its stadiums. Hence the need for a new "field of dreams" for the Bluebirds.

The memories of Ninian Park will never die, particularly with incredible photo archives such as the *Daily Mirror*'s, and also the memories of those Cardiff supporters over the years. As the new ground is constructed a stone's throw away from Ninian Park, the Cardiff City Stadium will produce its own memories in the future. One thing is for sure, being Cardiff City those memories will be good and bad but we will never forget the old girl from across the road.

"Goodbye Old Girl."
An aerial shot of Ninian Park in 1962.

1910 Cardiff acquire land in the Leckwith area of the city helped by Lord Ninian Crichton-Stuart MP. The ground is named Ninian Park. 1911 Gas and water are installed at the ground. The ground is used for Welsh international games. 1920 The Canton Stand is built. 1925 Tramlines are installed at the ground by the Cardiff Corporation. 1953 A record attendance for the club as 57,893 fans see Cardiff play Arsenal. 1958 The Empire Games come to the ground as it is used for show jumping. Wales beat Israel at the ground to secure a place in the 1958 World Cup in Sweden. 1959 The ground attendance record is broken as 62,000 fans see Wales against England. 1960 Floodlights are installed. 1961 Cardiff Rugby Club play at the ground. 1967 Welshman Howard Winstone fights for the world title at the ground against Vicente Saldivar. 1971 Cardiff City beat Real Madrid 1-0 in the Cup Winners' Cup. 1976 Bob Marley plays a gig at the ground. 1980 The Cardiff Tigers American Football team play at the ground. 1982 Pope John Paul II visits the ground for a mass to 58,000 Catholics. 1983 Rugby League comes to Cardiff with the Blue Dragons. 1985 Scotland manager Jock Stein dies at the ground following a heart attack. 2007 Cardiff lose the last game at the ground 3-0 to Ipswich Town. 2008 Ninian Park is demolished. 2009 Cardiff City's new ground opens with a friendly against Celtic. 2010 Welsh band Stereophonics play the first gig at the ground.

The Many Faces of Ninian Park

LEFT: Jack Petersen knocks out Heine Muller in their World Title fight at Ninian Park in 1933.

BELOW: Show jumping at the ground for the 1958 Empire Games held in Wales.

LEFT: The Grandstand in 1957.

BELOW: Wales' 1958 World Cup qualifying game against Israel at Ninian Park. John Charles moves in for goal. A win for Wales sent them to the 1958 World Cup in Sweden.

England keeper Gordon Banks punches the ball clear as Wales play England in the 1963 home internationals.

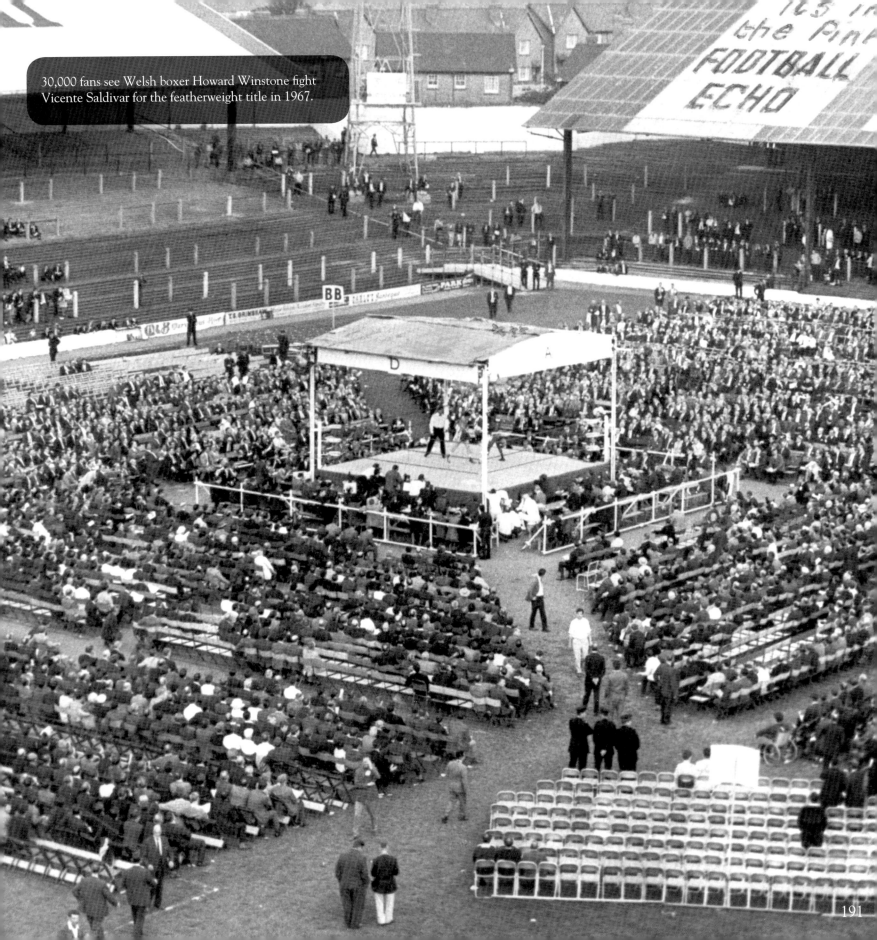

30,000 fans see Welsh boxer Howard Winstone fight Vicente Saldivar for the featherweight title in 1967.

191

Wales v Scotland, 1962. Wales captain John Charles and Scotland captain Eric Caldow lead out the teams at Ninian Park.

Money is thrown on to a blanket at the Wales v Scotland game at Ninian Park in 1966. The money was for the recent Aberfan disaster fund and £600 was raised at the game. The tragedy happened in October 1966 when a colliery spoil tip became unsteady in the mining village of Aberfan, due to wet weather, and slipped down the mountain onto the nearby school killing 116 children and 28 adults.

ABOVE: Singer Bob Marley played Ninian Park as part of his Rastaman Vibration tour in 1976.

LEFT: Life from the Bob Bank in 1970.

195

Even the children's enclosure was fenced in due to the recent rise in football violence. The fencing cost the club £4,000; it was a cost clubs like Cardiff could ill afford.

Cardiff City general manager Ron Jones looks on as the Rugby League posts are installed for the Blue Dragons at Ninian Park for the start of the Rugby League season. The venture only lasted a couple of seasons as the game fell out of favour with the Welsh public, with crowds being as low as 500.

ABOVE: The Blue Dragons clear the ball from a scrum during a game against Saltford.

BELOW: International Rugby League comes to the City in 1995 as Wales play Western Samoa.

A thumbs-up from the Bishop of Shrewsbury at Pope John Paul II's visit to Ninian Park in 1982. The papal visit attracted a crowd of over 58,000 for the mass service held at the ground.

The great Jock Stein who died at the ground after suffering a heart attack whilst managing his Scotland team against Wales in the 1986 World Cup qualifying campaign. Stein was 62 years old.

FAR LEFT: The old ground looking tired in 2005.

LEFT: The beginning of the end as demolition starts on the Grandstand.

BELOW: The Bob Bank is demolished.

The pitch is dug up before the bulldozers arrive.

The remains of the floodlights that witnessed so many European memories through the years.

203

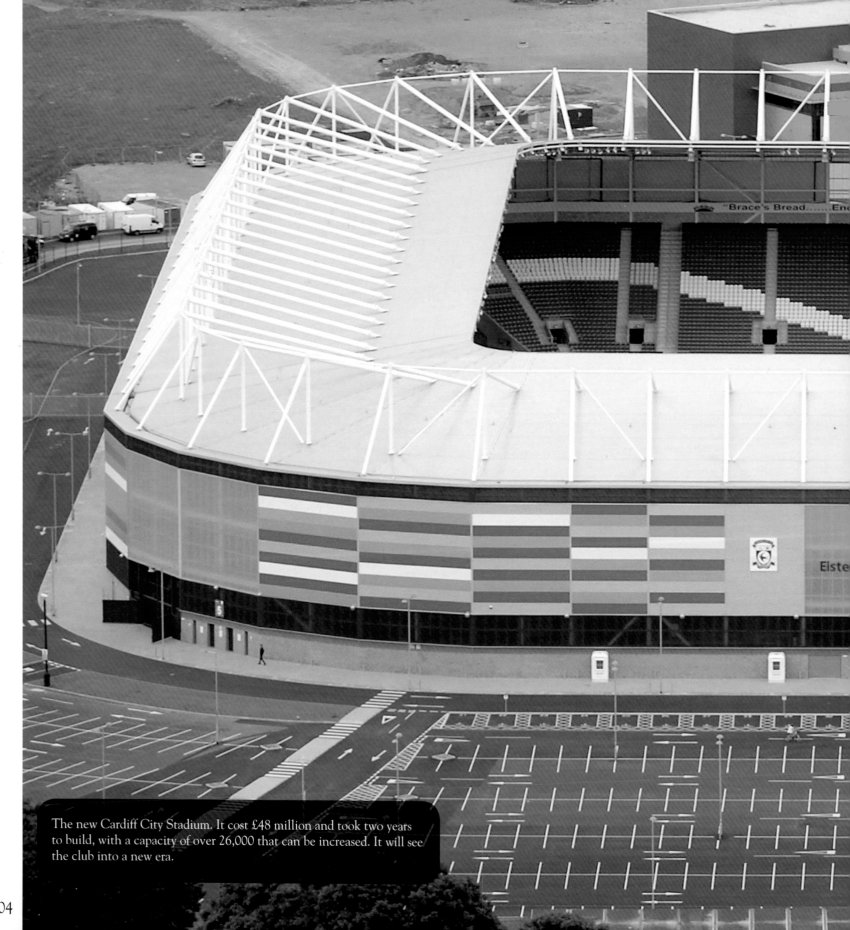

The new Cardiff City Stadium. It cost £48 million and took two years to build, with a capacity of over 26,000 that can be increased. It will see the club into a new era.

"Brace's Bread.......Enough said"   "Brace's Bread.......Enough said

NTON Stand

205

LEFT: Opening night at the new stadium, 22nd July 2009.

BELOW: Cardiff City v Glasgow Celtic and the first official game at the new ground.

Kelly Jones, lead singer with Welsh band Stereophonics, at the first gig played at the new stadium.

Acknowledgments

For Sally, Sophie and Jack for their help and support, and for putting up with my constant references to Cardiff City facts. Also to family and friends for their interest in the book.

I would like to thank Richard Havers for his guidance and enthusiasm in this project and, more importantly, for giving me the chance to write the book. All the people at Haynes Publishing who worked so hard in producing the end result. David Scripps and his team at Mirrorpix. Vito Inglese and Tony Woolway for their tireless efforts in supplying me with the photographs I asked for. Vanessa and Kevin Gardner for their advice and help along the way, along with David Instone.

Special thanks to Cardiff City legend Phil Dwyer for agreeing to get involved. Thanks also to Frank McGhee, Harry Millar, Monte Fresco, Kent Gavin and all those legendary *Daily Mirror* people who, without their knack for a photo or story, this book would not have been possible.

And finally all those Bluebird fans who have experienced this rollercoaster ride!!